GREAT CANADIAN GOLFERS

Stephen Drake

OVER
TIME
BOOKS

The Publisher: OverTime Books is an imprint of Éditions de la Montagne Verte

Library and Archives Canada Cataloguing in Publication

Drake, Stephen, 1960–
      Great Canadian golfers / Steve Drake.

Includes bibliographical references.
ISBN 978-1-897277-11-9

      1. Golfers—Canada—Biography. I. Title.

GV964.A1D73 2010   796.352092'271   C2009-906387-5

Project Director: J. Alexander Poulton
Editor: J. Alexander Poulton
Cover Image: Courtesy of Corbis Images;© Richard Wolowicz/ Icon SMI/Corbis: Mike Weir at the 2007 Presidents Cup Tournament at the Royal Montreal Golf Club (Sept. 26/07)

PC: 6

We acknowledge the financial support of the Government of Canada through the Book Publishing Industry Development Program (BPIDP) for our publishing activities.

Canadian Patrimoine
Heritage canadien

Contents

Introduction 5

Chapter 1:
Mike Weir: A Canadian Hero 10

Chapter 2:
A Masterful Victory 26

Chapter 3:
Stephen Ames: The Outspoken One 41

Chapter 4:
Lorie Kane: The Late Bloomer 56

Chapter 5:
Nelford and Leggatt: Promise Unfulfilled 69

Chapter 6:
The Girls from BC 87

Chapter 7:
Richard Zokol: "Disco Dick" 106

Chapter 8:
Dave Barr: Mr. Consistency 120

Chapter 9:
Jocelyne Bourassa: Rebel Golfer 135

Chapter 10:
Sandra Post: Our First Lady of Golf 150

Chapter 11:
George Knudson: The Natural Swinger 164

Chapter 12:
Stan Leonard: The Oldest Rookie 178

Chapter 13:
Al Balding: Canada's Forgotten Champion 192

Chapter 14:
Moe Norman: Canada's Golf Savant 206

Appendix:
Player Records 220

Notes on Sources 222

Dedication

To Joanne and Saul, Jim and Shemin,
thanks for everything.

Acknowledgments

The smaller the ball, the better the sportswriting.

–George Plimpton

Great Canadian golf writers like Lorne
Rubenstein, James Barclay and Arv Olson
provide plenty of evidence to support
Plimpton's theory. Thanks to all of you
for capturing our golfing history.

Introduction

We are a golfing nation. In 2006, the Royal Canadian Golf Association (RCGA) hired the polling company Ipsos Reid to find out how many people across the country play golf. After interviewing 20,000 citizens, the study found that 21.5% of Canadians took part in the sport, representing a national golfing population of 5.95 million people.

Canada's participation rate is one of the highest in the world (only 9% of the American population plays golf). We also pay out a lot of money on golf-related expenditures—the report concluded the golfing community in Canada spends about $13 billion each year.

Golf has been around in Canada since before we were even a country. Records show that in 1854 a 16-year-old Scottish sailor named William Dibman found the Plains of Abraham the ideal place to hit some golf shots.

Canadians formed private golf clubs in the early 1870s, 15 years before the first association was established in the United States. It was an obscure sport in our country in those days, but in the early 1900s the game expanded across Canada.

George S. Lyon was our first great golf champion. Lyon won eight national amateur titles playing out of the Toronto Rosedale Club; he won a gold medal in golf in the 1904 St. Louis Olympics. (He celebrated the victory by walking through the clubhouse on his hands.)

Earlier that summer the first Canadian Open golf tournament was held. It remains the third oldest national tournament in the world, trailing only the British and U.S. Opens.

Most of our early golfing heroes were amateur players. Besides Lyon, there was Dorothy Campbell Hurd Howe who won three Canadian ladies titles, three British ladies championships and three U.S. ladies titles between 1901 and 1924. Ada Mackenzie won five Canadian Amateur titles between 1919 and 1935. In 1924, Mackenzie founded a golf club in Toronto that was exclusively for women, the first of its kind in North America.

The lineage of great Canadian amateur players continued through the years. Gary Cowan, Gail Moore, Marilyn Palmer O'Connor, Doug Roxburgh and Cathy Sherk, found success both at home and abroad.

In the professional ranks, Canadian triumphs have been scarce. The last Canuck to win our national championship was Pat Fletcher in 1954. Over the years much hand wringing and blame has been passed around, as well as many theories on why a country that so passionately plays the sport has been able to produce so few professional champions.

Indeed, we have had only a handful of players who have been successful on the PGA and LPGA Tours. The link between them exemplifies the tightness of the golfing community in our country. Al Balding and Stan Leonard were the first Canadians to find success on the PGA Tour (a young George Knudson caddied for both and learned what was required to become a touring professional).

Jim Nelford was one of the first Canadians to win a golfing scholarship at an American university. Nelford told his golf coach at Brigham Young University that he should give a tryout to a kid from Vancouver named Richard Zokol. As a veteran PGA player, it was Zokol who offered advice to Mike Weir, then a struggling BYU alumni trying to make it on to the Tour.

On the women's side, Sandra Post and Jocelyn Bourassa, Canada's first LPGA players, devoted their post-competitive careers to growing the sport. Post established a golfing academy for women and has been advocate for female participation in the sport. Bourassa was the executive director of the du Maurier Classic for 20 years and started a developmental tour for Canadian women. The next generation of Canuck stars— Gail Graham, Lisa Walters, Dawn Coe-Jones and Lorie Kane—all have said Bourassa made a huge contribution in their progression as touring pros.

As the 2009 golf season ended, Canadians have found little recent success on the PGA or LPGA tours. Mike Weir has not won a tournament since 2007. Stephen Ames was in a similar drought until winning the last PGA event on the 2009 calendar. Weir will turn 40 in 2010 and Ames will be 46. Lorie Kane is nearing retirement—the best Canadian LPGA player is Angela Sharp who is still looking for a top result in her fifth year on the women's circuit.

A decade after the RCGA started a new developmental program to push players to the top level of the sport it seems there is some reason for optimism. Nick Taylor and Matt Hill are the two top-ranked amateur players in the world. Taylor, a student at the University of Washington won four NCAA tournaments in 2009 and was the best amateur at the U.S. Open.

Hill of Bright Groves, Ontario, Weir's hometown, has victories in eight NCAA events in his collegiate career at North Carolina State. This year he won the Jack Nicklaus Award as the NCAA college player of the year. Another former top amateur, Chris Baryla from Vernon, BC, won a Nationwide Tour title in 2009. Baryla and Graham DeLaet from Weyburn, Saskatchewan, who tied for eighth at the six-round PGA Tour qualifying tournament at the end of 2009, will join Weir and Ames on the PGA circuit in 2010.

On the women's side, Kelowna's Samantha Richdale won two Futures Tour events in 2009 and clinched a spot on the LPGA Tour for 2010. Jennifer Kirby, an 18-year-old from Paris, Ontario, has already won a Canadian amateur title and is considered the next up-and-coming great player.

Still, it will be a big jump for the new crop of Canadian talent to find the kind of success that Weir and Kane have enjoyed in the professional ranks. It took Weir years of scraping by on second-tier circuits to make it to the PGA Tour, and Kane didn't become a full-time player on the LPGA Tour until she was 33 years old.

"It's a big hump to get over," summed up Weir about transforming amateur success to reaching golf's top level. "It took me six years to do it."

Let's hope Canadian fans won't have to wait that long to see one of their own make it to the top of the leaderboard.

Chapter One

Mike Weir

A Canadian Hero

Born Sarnia, Ontario, 1970–

When Canadians are asked to list our country's greatest athletes, the conversation often starts and ends with hockey—Rocket Richard, Gordie Howe, Bobby Orr, Guy Lafleur, Wayne Gretzky, Mario Lemieux and Sidney Crosby. But if the discussion is widened to include other sports, another equally impressive list emerges: Donovan Bailey, Steve Nash, Larry Walker, Justin Morneau, the late Gilles Villeneuve, Gaétan Boucher, Nancy Greene and Cindy Klassen come to mind.

Perhaps the greatest individual achievement in the last 25 years of Canadian sport, however, came in 2003 when Mike Weir won the Masters (more on Weir's victory in the next chapter). An entire nation put the NHL schedule aside to watch the lefthander from Brights Grove, Ontario, sink a seven-foot putt on the 18th hole to force a playoff with Len Mattiace. A tap-in putt on the first playoff hole sealed the deal, and Weir became the first Canadian male to ever win a professional major championship.

Mike Weir has been far from a one-hit wonder. He has won eight times on the PGA Tour and has finished in the top 10 in all four of the major championships. He has over $27 million in career earnings and stands 11th on the all-time money list. In 1999, he became the first Canadian in 45 years to win a PGA tournament on home soil when he prevailed at the Air Canada Championship in Surrey, BC. At the 2004 Canadian Open he lost a heart-breaking playoff to Vijay Singh and came that close to bringing home the title for the first time since 1954 when Pat Fletcher won the event in Vancouver.

At first glance, Weir is an unimposing sports hero. He stands just five-foot-nine and weighs a slight 155 pounds. Upon closer inspection, however, his slim frame consists of sinew and muscle, crafted through hours in the gym. He is all business on the golf course—he plays with a determined look in his eyes, a pursed mouth and quick gait.

Brights Grove is a small community just north of Sarnia on the shores of Lake Huron. Mike Weir was eight years old when his father, Rich, took him to play golf for the first time at a nine-hole, par-28 course at the Holiday Inn Golf Club. He was a lefty from the get-go, and fortunately, a neighbour had a set of old left-handed clubs kicking around to get him started.

At age 10, the Weir family moved to a home across the street from the Huron Oaks Golf Club, and the young Weir quickly became a golf course rat. Weir and his friends played almost every day through the summer. Even though he was small in stature (he didn't reach five feet until his 14th birthday), Weir was a determined athlete and a fierce competitor.

Playing golf was not the only sport Weir loved. He played hockey and delighted in nailing much bigger opponents into the boards. He was even a better baseball player. He pitched and also played first base and catcher. Volleyball, table tennis, basketball and swimming were all part of his sporting repertoire.

In September 1981, Jack Nicklaus played an exhibition with Steve Bennett, the club pro at Huron Oaks. An 11-year-old Mike Weir followed Nicklaus all around the back nine, watching how the great Nicklaus carried himself and how he prepared for each shot. The Golden Bear took every stroke seriously, and it was that example that Weir decided to emulate.

At a junior tournament, he shot a 70 to beat golfers as much as five year older than he was. Weir was 14 when he began questioning the consistency of his swing and wondered if he should play right-handed. He decided to seek advice from Nicklaus and wrote him a brief note: "I want to be a professional golfer. I play left-handed. Do you think I should switch?"

A month later he received a short reply: "I have always believed that a left-handed player is better off sticking with his natural swing." From that point on, Weir never questioned his swing; instead he rededicated himself to the game, practicing throughout the winter in the family's garage.

In 1985, Weir finished second at the Ontario Junior championship, won two other tournaments and was in the top 10 in all 15 events he entered. The next year, he added four more titles, playing in a popular junior series called the Tyson Tour, and later in the year he won the Canadian Juvenile championship in Edmonton.

With such an impressive resume, 10 American universities were interested in the young Canadian. At 17, he finished tied for fourth at an American junior event—four shots behind Phil

Mickelson, another left-hander who had been the number-one-ranked junior in the U.S. the year before.

A few weeks later, Weir made it through two rounds of the U.S. Junior championship (a match play format) at Vail, Colorado. Karl Tucker, the golf coach at Brigham Young University (BYU) was impressed with the young Canuck. Tucker had coached Canadian players Jim Nelford, Richard Zokol and Brent Franklin. Zokol vouched for Weir's character and told Tucker he was fine golfer.

After visiting five other universities, Weir chose BYU. He won a tournament in his freshman year and then returned home to play in amateur events. Weir qualified for his first Canadian Open at Glen Abbey and shot 80–71 to miss the cut. He also won the Ontario Amateur (a title he would win for the second time two years later).

Weir wasn't able to win a tournament in his sophomore year at BYU, but his game improved. He added two more event titles before graduating in 1992 as an All-American selection, and he finished second at consecutive Canadian Amateur Championships in 1991 and 1992.

Weir tried his first shot at qualifying for the PGA Tour in 1993 and stalled during the second qualifying stage. He settled for the Canadian Tour instead, a respected training ground for young professionals. By this time, Weir had married his college sweetheart, Bricia Rodriguez, and the young couple decided to settle down in Salt Lake City.

They were on the road so much for the next four years that instead of leasing an apartment, they rented a storage unit for their belongings. Weir played in Australia, Asia, Europe and across Canada. When they returned home to Salt Lake City, they leased an apartment.

Weir was totally focused on his goal of not only making the PGA Tour but of becoming a successful pro as well. In 1994, he again failed at qualifying school. "I never thought of giving up," Weir said. "I always knew I'd find a way."

After playing steady golf in both Australia and Asia in 1995, Weir didn't get through PGA qualifying (his third attempt). His failure wasn't due to lack of commitment. He practiced for hours and kept his body flexible and strong through daily workouts. His longtime mentor, Richard Zokol, encouraged Weir to get some help with his swing. He ended up finding Mike Wilson, an instructor based out of Palm Springs. The two worked to get Weir to elevate his shots so he could control his long irons. The change began to pay off in 1996 at the PGA Tour's Greater Vancouver Open (as a Canadian, Weir received an exemption to play). Weir stayed in contention until the last hole when his approach shot found water. Still, Weir finished fifth playing against a PGA field.

In 1997, he won two events on the Canadian Tour. In seven tournaments he earned $80,698 to become the first Canadian in eight years to win the money title. In the fall, he made his sixth trip to the PGA qualifying school and for the first time advanced to the final stage.

During the first four days of the six-round ordeal, Weir stayed close to the top, never shooting worse than 72. A fifth round 71 put him at six under par, near the leaderboard, but still on the bubble. The last round came down to a pair of critical birdies on the finishing holes. He had shot another 71, but with no scoreboards on the course, Weir had no way of knowing whether he had qualified for the Tour.

Weir had tied for 26th place at seven under, good enough to get in. Weir cried with relief when told by a reporter from the Golf Channel that he had qualified. "That's when the emotions hit me, because it was a dream come true, a dream I'd had since I was kid first taking up the game."

Not surprisingly, he struggled his first year out on the Tour, missing the cut in 14 of the first

26 tournaments he played. By the time he came to the last tournament, he was 126th on the money list. Only the top 125 money-winners get to play on the Tour the next year. Weir struggled at the season-ending Walt Disney World Classic and dropped to 131st on the money list, earning $218,967.

By not dropping below 150th in earnings, Weir at least avoided the first two rounds of qualifying school and went directly to the final stage. After shooting an opening round 75 on the first day of Q-school, Weir switched back to an old putter and went 27-under par for the remaining four rounds. He ended up winning the tournament, setting himself up nicely for the 1999 season.

With new confidence and the rookie jitters behind him, Weir finally began to contend on the Tour. He was 13th in Tucson and then fifth at the BellSouth Classic in Atlanta. At the Western Open he played in the final grouping with Tiger Woods and finished second, cashing a cheque for $270,000—more than he had made all the previous season. Perhaps more encouragingly, Weir wasn't intimidated playing the final round with Woods—he actually outscored the world's best player with a round of 70 (Woods shot a 71).

Weir went overseas a week before the British Open and qualified for the tournament by shooting rounds of 71 and 66. The weather at Carnoustie in Scotland turned nasty as the Open began. Facing wind gusts up to 45 kilometers per hour, Weir shot an 83, his worst round of golf as a professional player. The next day the conditions weren't much better, but Weir rallied to shoot a 72 and, incredibly, made the cut. He finished in 37th place, a promising first step in his initial adventure with "links" golf. Links courses are built on sandy soil, whether seaside or not, and are buffeted by strong winds. A links course plays firm and fast, often with crusty fairways and greens that feature many knolls and knobs to create odd bounces and angles. A links course is relatively treeless with a native rough that is tall and thick.

A month later Weir was on the front page of sports sections across Canada. After three rounds of the PGA championship, he was the co-leader with Tiger Woods. Weir had fashioned three wonderful rounds of 68-68-69 to earn the right to again go toe-to-toe with Woods in the final grouping. It was only his third major championship, and Weir knew whatever happened would be a great learning experience. His putter didn't work on Sunday, he missed short par-saving putts early in the round and tumbled out of contention. Even as he slipped to 10th place, Weir kept his eyes on Woods and watched how he gutted out yet another major championship.

"No question about it, it was painful," said Weir years later when asked about the meltdown. "I remember feeling after nine holes just kind of spacey, just spun out. I couldn't believe what was going on. I was striking the ball well, but I had no feel on the greens, and I was frustrated with all the commotion, playing with Tiger, people running when you're hitting. I wasn't ready for that. So, you learn from that."

Three weeks later, Weir was back in Canada at the Air Canada Championship (formerly the Greater Vancouver Open). He had finished fifth at the tournament in 1996 and 1998 and liked the Northview Golf and Country Club. He shot 68-70-64 and was tied for fourth, two shots behind the leader Fred Funk, heading into the final round.

After a bogey on the first hole, Weir made four straight birdies on the front nine. After birdies on the 10th and 12th holes, the young Canadian moved into contention. On the par-four 14th, Weir was faced with a second shot of 159 yards to the pin. His shot landed 20 feet short of the hole and then rolled in for an eagle.

It was the turning point. Weir birdied the 16th to take a three-shot lead over Funk. After consecutive birdies, Funk pulled to within one shot of the crowd favourite. Weir battled his nerves to par the final hole and then watched as Funk failed to birdie the 18th. Weir had won his first PGA title, becoming only the sixth left-hander to win in Tour history.

Weir's breakthrough season continued with a tie for 10th at the BC Open and a third place finish at the Michelob Championship. It was his seventh top-10 finish of the year. In 30 tournaments, Weir had won almost $1.5 million to finish 23rd on the money list. For the first time in his career, he didn't have to worry about a trip back to the PGA qualifying tournament.

In 2000, Weir continued to add more top-10 finishes to his golfing portfolio. For the first time in 10 attempts he made the cut at the Canadian Open, then after a three-week break, he lost in a playoff to David Toms at the Michelob event.

Weir's consistent play earned him a spot on the Presidents Cup team, an event that pits the 12 best International, but non-European players against the 12 best American-born players. The U.S. was hosting the 2000 tournament in Virginia. The home side, with Tiger Woods, Phil Mickelson, David Duval and David Love III were highly favoured and ended up trouncing the visitors by 10 points. Weir, however, won three out of a possible five points and was the top player on the International team.

Weir had earned more than $1.5 million in 2000 with the season-ending World Golf Championship still on the calendar. The event with the biggest prize of the year was held in Spain, and Weir stayed in contention after the first round by shooting a four-under 68. After shooting a disappointing 75 on Friday, Weir made a minor adjustment to his posture and was able to drop his score to 65 to move within one shot of the lead.

Weir made four birdies on the front nine to take a three-shot advantage heading home. On the back nine, his lead shrunk to a single shot. The 17th hole was the hardest on the course, all the contenders, including Tiger Woods found the water, but Weir avoided trouble and secured a par. His final round 69 was enough for a two-shot victory, a three-year exemption on the PGA Tour and a cheque for $1 million that vaulted him into sixth place on the money list. In January, he received one of the highest honours of his young career when he was named the Canadian Press Male Athlete of the Year.

Weir wouldn't add to his PGA Tour win total until the last event of 2001. He came close with runner-up finishes at the Doral and BellSouth events, but didn't contend at any of the majors. At the season-ending Tour Championship in Houston, Weir started the final round two shots behind the leader, but shot a 68 to get into a four-way playoff. On the first extra hole he hit a wedge to within five feet of the hole and sank the birdie putt to win his third career title. The victory moved him up to 11th place on the money list.

Weir's next Tour title came at the start of the magical 2003 season. He won the Bob Hope Chrysler Classic by two strokes over Jay Haas and three weeks later added another win at the Nissan Open by defeating Charles Howell III in a playoff. Then came the Masters title two months later, followed by a third place finish at the U.S. Open and a seventh place tie at the PGA Championship.

Weir's run moved him up to third in the official World Golf Rankings and concluded the most remarkable season ever turned in by a Canadian player on the PGA circuit. The little lefty banked $4.9 million to finish sixth on the money list and was awarded the Lou Marsh Trophy as outstanding Canadian athlete.

If 2003 provided the most jubilant moment in Weir's golfing career, then the 2004 season would be perhaps the most disappointing. Canadians were hoping that a native son would finally come through to win their national tournament. It had been 50 years since a Canadian had captured the title, and with Weir in his prime, Canadian golf fans hoped the long drought would end.

Weir won his seventh career PGA title in the early part of 2004, defending his Nissan Open title. At Glen Abbey, Weir was playing well and shot a second round 65 to grab the lead. Despite having two three-putts on the last nine holes, Weir held on to top spot until the tournament's 72nd hole when Vijay Singh pulled into a first-place tie.

Singh was having an historic season—he would win nine times and bank over $11 million. Still, Weir had a chance to win the Canadian Open outright on the last hole, but his eight-foot putt curled away from the cup.

Thousands of spectators had lined the 18th, wearing hockey jerseys and yelling so loudly that Weir had to open his mouth and yawn to pop his ears. On the second playoff hole, Weir had another chance to close out the tourney, but he missed a six-footer. On the next hole, Singh almost reluctantly took the title. He later apologized to the fans and Weir at the trophy presentation.

"I know how hard it is to win at home, especially with the crowd as vocal as what they were out there," said the Fijian afterwards. "Towards the end, they were really cheering for Mike. I hope they didn't get to him, but in my mind they must have affected him one way or the other."

"It was really special," said a tearful Weir at this press conference after. "I'll always remember this week no matter what I do the rest of my career."

Weir finished a solid 16th on the money list in 2004, but for the better part of the next three seasons the veteran golfer struggled. He dropped to 73rd in earnings in 2005, rebounded slightly to 42nd the next year and looked destined for another lost season before winning the Fry's Electronic Open, the last event of 2007. His eighth PGA victory tied him with George Knudson for the most Tour victories by a Canadian.

Weir had received a big shot of confidence the month before at the Presidents Cup at the Royal Montreal Golf Club. With thousands of home supporters cheering him on, Weir defeated Tiger Woods on the last day of the event. The match play victory was a consolation prize for the International team who had been overwhelmed by the American side over the three-day competition. But when Weir won the last two holes to defeat Woods, the crowd chanted "Mike! Mike! Mike!"

The Canadian had won only one point for his team in a losing cause, but what a point it was.

"I told him I was proud of how he handled himself," said Woods. "He had to carry an entire country on his shoulders. Not too many people can play as well as he did. He handled it magnificently."

Mike Weir has not won on the PGA Tour since 2007. He remains, however, a consistent top-10 player. In 2008, he finished 14th on the money list, earning just over $3 million. In 2009, he added five more top 10s including a second place finish at Pebble Beach and a third at the Bob Hope Classic.

And even though Weir turns 40 in May 2010, he is still capable of conjuring some of the magic of tourneys past. At the 2009 U.S. Open, Weir opened with a 64 and then stayed near the top of the leaderboard with a second round 70. However, a pair of 74s over the final two rounds dropped him to 10th place.

Weir finished 26th on the money list in 2009 and played in his fourth Presidents Cup. He remains Canada's best golfer.

Chapter Two

A Masterful Victory

Winning a major championship in professional golf isn't a guarantee of greatness, but no player can be considered great unless he wins at least one Masters, U.S. Open, British Open or PGA title.

Just before Mike Weir prevailed at Augusta in 2003, he was already considered a good golfer—the winner of several tournaments, a high finisher on the money list—a consistent and well-respected competitor. But when Weir won the green jacket, he elevated his game to another level; he had become a champion of a major tournament.

There was an added layer to Weir's victory. He became the first Canadian male to win a major, joining Sandra Post, the U.S. Women's Open titleholder in 1968 as the only players from north of the 49th parallel to win one of the big ones.

Weir's march to the Masters title was much more celebrated than Post's win over 30 years earlier. The LPGA Tour was still in its infancy. Post's victory wasn't televised and the depth of the women's field was much thinner than it is today.

The Masters is the only major championship played on the same course each year, establishing a lineage of tradition unsurpassed in professional golf. The courses in Scotland and England may be older, but all the best players in the world only started to compete in the British Open when Arnold Palmer began making the then expensive trip across the Atlantic in the 1960s.

In 1931, a year after Bobby Jones won his historic Grand Slam (in those days the four events were the U.S. and British Open, plus the U.S. and British Amateur), he and his friend Clifford Roberts, a New York stockbroker, purchased a piece of property in Augusta, Georgia. The goal was to construct one of the finest golf courses in the world. Even though the project started in the middle of an economic downturn, the club opened in 1933, and a year later an invitational tournament called the Masters was held for the first time.

Jones, one of the most popular sports stars in America, was the club's president, and Roberts was the chairman. The charisma of Jones combined with the business acumen of Roberts guaranteed the success of the club, and the Masters became an important tournament on the golfing calendar.

It wasn't until after World War II that the tournament became a major, rivaling the importance of the U.S. Open on the golfing calendar. President Dwight D. Eisenhower was the club's most famous member, and Roberts arranged for the construction of a cottage on the grounds for Ike's exclusive use.

The popularity of golf had reached new levels with the emergence of Palmer and then Jack Nicklaus in the 1960s and '70s. And the importance of the Masters grew with the sport. With the advent of television, the look and feel of Augusta National was brought into American homes for the first time. The Masters is perhaps played in the most physically beautiful backdrop in all of sports. The dazzling display of dogwoods and azaleas in bloom has become symbolic with the return of spring.

The Masters is the only golf event where practice rounds are actually attended by more people than the four tournament rounds. Through a ticket lottery system, the club allows 35,000 people on the course to watch the best golfers in the world prepare for the rigors of the tourney. Only 25,000 badges are sold for the actual tournament.

There is no gouging at the Masters. Parking is free, and the concession prices are half of what you'd pay at an NFL game. Masters memorabilia is only sold at the tournament, again at reasonable prices. The club also controls the telecast of the event. Commercial time is extremely limited—only four minutes of advertising per hour is allowed. There are no electronic scoreboards at the Masters; people hidden behind the boards make changes manually. There is no corporate presence; advertising is forbidden on the grounds; and beverages are poured into green Masters paper cups.

Augusta National is a storied place. Magnolia Lane, a 200-metre long street leading from Gate Two to the clubhouse is one of the most celebrated strips of roadway in the world. The white clubhouse at the end of the lane is three-stories high. It contains a library with shelves of books on golf dating back to the 19th century; the room is also used to host the Champions Dinner and the Victory Dinner during Masters week.

The clubhouse also contains the champion's dressing room, reserved for past winners. It is a sanctuary, off-limits to the press. The locker room downstairs is open to the media. There are historic pictures on every wall, photos of the course and clubhouse through the years, past champions and important club members.

Ninety-eight cabins are located close to the main buildings. Most of them are two-bedroom cottages available to the 300 members to rent when they come to the club or to reserve for the Masters. Ike's Cabin, the cottage specially built for President Eisenhower when he was in office and Butler Cabin, is known to television viewers as the place where the awards ceremony is held and the winner interviewed.

Next to the clubhouse is a par-three course, which is one of the most beautiful places on the grounds. The par-three tournament is part of the Masters tradition. There is also a jinx associated with the event—no player has ever won the par-three tourney and the Masters in the same year.

Through decades of televised coverage, Augusta National has become the most famous golf course in the world. The continuity of the Masters brings the same landmarks into our living rooms each year. Amens Corner, Rae's Creek, Sarazen Bridge...have all become as familiar as the layout at our local pitch and putt.

However, in 2003, Augusta National's image was in poor order. For the previous 10 months a women's rights activist named Martha Burkes had been leading a crusade against the club's policy of men-only membership. Burkes had sent an open letter to club chairman William "Hootie" Johnson insisting that the club open its doors to women. Johnson mishandled the pressure tactics of Burkes, and much of the public's sentiment was directed against the club's elite, powerful membership. As the tournament drew nearer, Burkes stated that there could be protests at Augusta if the club's policy didn't change.

The weather was also nasty in 2003. A week of heavy rain had left the course sodden, forcing the postponement of Thursday's opening round. To combat the soggy conditions, grounds-keepers were forced to spread a pungent drying agent over the course. Augusta National literally stunk.

Mike Weir headed into the Masters as the winner of two PGA events in 2003, but had missed the cut at the BellSouth Classic the week before. It was his fourth Masters, and heading into the tournament, he was having his best season on the Tour. Weir had enjoyed some good rounds at Augusta in the past but had never strung together a successful enough run through a whole tournament.

With Thursday's opening round postponed, the golfers faced an endurance test on Friday. Play started early in the morning with the hope that most of the field would be able to get in 36 holes by nightfall.

Weir's first round took over five hours to play. He remained bogey-free until the 18th when he missed a five-foot putt. His two-under 70 put him four strokes behind the leader Darren Clarke. But Weir was not the only one suffering; the cold, sodden conditions took their toll on many in the field—Woods shot a 76, Ernie Els a 79. Even the great Jack Nicklaus shot 85, the worst score of his 43 years on the PGA Tour.

At the halfway point of the second round, Weir began to turn things around, looking comfortable on the course and playing smart, strategic golf. Three consecutive birdies mid-round moved him up the leaderboard. The horn blew to suspend play at 7:26 PM, but Weir chose to finish his 30th hole of the day. He was on a roll and wanted to keep going. It turned out to be the right decision after he rolled in a six-foot birdie putt to get to six-under-par, two shots up on the rest of the field.

"It would have been nice to finish," Weir said at the media center later. "But I'm glad that we got in as many holes as we could. I thought that we'd get twenty-seven in, but we got thirty."

At 8:45 AM the next morning, play resumed with Weir having six holes remaining to complete his second round. A nice up and down out of a bunker saved par, but then a bogey on the fifth knocked him down to five-under. The Canadian struggled with his shot-making, and only clutch putts on the next two holes kept him from sliding closer to the rest of the field.

A birdie-par on the next two holes and the first two rounds were done. Weir had shot 70-68 to finish four shots ahead of leader Darren Clarke who slipped to a 76 after his opening 66. The left-hander was suddenly in demand as the media clued in that Weir had a chance to win the tournament.

"I'm not thinking about numbers," summed up Weir. "Not at all. I'll just keep grinding. I'll warm up the same way for this afternoon and do some stretching. I feel a little tight."

A few hours later Weir was paired with Clarke, and the two began their third round. Woods had barely made the cut and was 11 shots off the lead. A birdie on the second hole dropped Weir to seven-under, but he gave that back when he missed an eight-footer on the fifth hole.

A great approach shot on the seventh hole set up another birdie, but on the ninth hole he missed a five-footer to save par. Weir was treading water, but Clarke shot a two-over-par 38 on the front nine to fall six shots behind. The amateur Ricky Barnes was now second, four shots behind Weir.

In the distance, however, lurked a Tiger. Woods had birdied four of his first 10 holes in the third round and now trailed Weir by seven shots. On the 11th hole, Weir faced serious trouble for the first time. He buried his second shot in the bank between the water and the green. His caddie, Brennan Little, wanted him to take a one-shot penalty, hit the ball from the drop area and play for a bogey.

Weir saw an opportunity to get on the green by knocking the sharp edge of his pitching wedge against the soil under the ball. After a brief discussion with Little, Weir grabbed the wedge and took a mighty slash at the ball. It popped out, running 15 feet from the hole. After barely missing the par putt, Weir ended up taking a "good bogey."

On the next hole, Weir survived yet another tricky six-footer for par. Tiger had kept the pressure on; by going five-under in the third round, he now trailed by only five shots. There was more trouble for Weir on the 13th, another bogey after his second shot plopped into Rae's Creek. A birdie on the 15th helped a little, but he gave it back with a bogey on 17. Weir ended up shooting a 75 and was at 213 after three rounds.

The new leader was Jeff Maggert, who shot a 66. His three-round total of five-under par 211 put him two shots ahead of Weir. Woods also shot 66 and was at 215.

When Weir was asked about the round, he replied: "Obviously, I'm not real happy, but I still have a chance to win. I have to look at it like that. That was my bad round, I hope."

After sleeping 10 straight hours, Weir was ready for Sunday's final round. An estimated television audience of two million Canadians tuned in hoping to see history made that afternoon. Millions more Americans were watching, expecting Tiger Woods to complete his climb up the leaderboard and defend his Masters title.

Weir and Maggert were the last twosome on the course. A large crowd followed the tournament leaders throughout the afternoon, but an even larger gallery stuck with Tiger and José Maria Olazabal, expecting Woods to make a charge.

On the first hole, Weir sank a tricky three-footer for par. On the second he had a tap-in birdie putt to get to four-under. Maggert settled for par. Woods, playing two groups ahead of the leaders, brought his score down to two-under before unravelling on the short, but tricky 330-yard third hole. Woods gambled and decided to go for the flag off the tee box. The drive went right, into the azaleas; it took him four shots to get on the green. Two putts and a double-bogey later, Woods was out of contention.

The third hole also fouled up Maggert. A normally reliable sand player, the tourney leader watched in horror as the ball caught the lip of the bunker and ricocheted back toward him, hitting him in the chest. A two-stroke penalty was imposed, and Maggert had to hole a 10-footer for a triple-bogey.

In a few short minutes, Weir had opened up a two-stroke lead. Woods, perhaps the best golfer in history was no longer a factor. Things seemed to be heading in the right direction for the 32-year-old Canadian.

On the fourth, Maggert gained a stroke with a birdie; Weir was only up by a single shot. On the sixth, Weir regained the two-stroke lead with his second birdie of the afternoon. After hooking his drive on the seventh, Weir hit his third shot within a foot of the cup, saving par. He had to scramble to make par on the eighth, before settling down for a routine par on nine.

At the turn (as they say in golf parlance), Weir was leading the tournament at five-under. The new threat was Len Mattiace, who was four-under for the day and only one stroke behind the leader. Weir parred the 10th, but Mattiace had eagled the 13th and now led by one stroke. Maggert, who was at four-under, fell apart on the 12th, hitting two shots into Rae's Creek. It had come down to a two-man duel for the championship.

On the par-five 15th hole, Mattiace birdied, going two shots up on Weir. The left-hander replied with a birdie of his own on the 13th, but Mattiace was red-hot. Another birdie on 16 put him two up again.

After a par on 14, Weir had an opportunity to gain a stroke on the par-five 15th. His tee shot ended up in the left rough, and facing a 240-yard second shot, Weir laid up short of the green. With 91 yards left, Weir hit a perfect sand wedge within two feet of the hole. The crowd gave him a standing ovation as the Canadian walked up to the green to tap in his birdie putt.

A few seconds later the cheers turned into a gasp as the scoreboard posted a Mattiace bogey on 18. With three holes left, Weir was tied for the lead at seven-under par. At the par-three 16th hole, Weir's tee shot finished 10 feet right of the hole—a safe two-putt, and he remained the co-leader.

After a perfect tee shot on 17, Weir was left with 147 yards to the hole. His second shot came up 35 feet left of the pin. Weir's birdie attempt rolled three feet past the hole, but he cleanly sank the par putt.

Birdie to win and par for a playoff. As he walked to the 18th tee, he had to shoot either one of those or he was out. His drive was good— on the left side of the fairway, leaving him with 200 yards to the green. Weir's four-iron approach landed short of the hill protecting the hole. The ball ended up rolling back to where it landed, some 45 feet to the pin.

With so much on the line, Weir left his first putt seven feet short of the hole. The gallery fell silent, and Weir wasted no time sizing up the work that was left. After two practice strokes, he hit the putt firmly; the ball ran true and fell into the middle of the cup.

It was the biggest putt of his life. "It was just a gut-wrenching day, [with] a lot of comeback putts that I needed to make and was able to make," Weir said later. "To do that coming down the stretch, knowing what a great score Len's had today, that's what I'm really proud of. I wouldn't wish that last putt on 18 on anybody."

The playoff began on the 10th hole. Both Mattiace and Weir hit solid tee shots. Weir grabbed the advantage when Mattiace hooked his six-iron far left behind a pine tree. Weir's approach was on the green, 45-feet from the pin.

The pressure was on Mattiace to pull off a great shot, but instead his pitch flew through the rough and ran 25 feet past the hole. Weir's birdie attempt slid six-feet by the hole. Mattiace's par putt then ran 18 feet past the hole; he also missed his bogey putt. Weir was left with two putts for the Masters title, and he used both to seal the victory.

As the crowd filled the spring air with a thundering ovation, the Canadian lefty managed only to lift his arms half-heartedly in victory. The weight of his achievement had hit home. After receiving congratulations from family and friends on the 18th green, Weir sank heavily into the front seat of his golf cart. He simply needed refuge for a moment from all that was happening around him. He covered his face with his hands and quietly sobbed. His father, Rich, was in the back seat. He leaned over and wrapped his arms around his son. "That's all right, Mike," his father said. "Let it all out. It's okay."

An entire nation had held its breath as Weir sank one pivotal putt after another throughout the final round. After receiving the green jacket from Tiger Woods and being the guest of honour at the post-Masters dinner, it was just after midnight when the Canadian hero quietly snuck a dozen or so beers from the fridge at Augusta National and celebrated with his group back at the house he had rented.

A day later he returned to Canada to launch a new line of golf accessories in Toronto. At a news conference he reflected on what had happened. "You know, I was playing out there yesterday, and it was nerve-racking, for sure," he chuckled. "But I was having fun, too. Butch [his caddie] and I were laughing at how exciting it was. We were looking around, looking at all the people, and saying, 'This is cool! This is what we dreamed about as kids, walking up 18 with a chance to win the Masters.'"

Chapter Three

Stephen Ames
The Outspoken One

Born San Fernando, Trinidad and Tobago, 1964–

In the corporate world of professional golf, most players go about their business in well, a business-like manner. This partially explains the popularity of John Daly, who despite his many excesses and poor judgment is still one of the most beloved characters on the PGA circuit. Daly has never seemed too worried about upsetting sponsors, the PGA establishment or his fellow players. This makes Daly interesting to the media because they are not going to get the well-coached corporate line when they ask him questions.

Calgary's Stephen Ames, the transplanted Canadian from Trinidad and Tobago, is nothing like John Daly. No booze-ups, multiple divorces or weight problems. But, like Daly, when Ames is asked a question, he doesn't hold much back in his reply.

A sampling of Stephen Ames sound bites:

- On receiving an invitation to play the Masters after winning the Tournament Players Championship in March 2006: "I had no plans of playing at Augusta. My priorities have always been family first. If it comes down to that, it's probably going to be a two-week vacation...I'd rather go on vacation, to be truthful."

- A month earlier he provoked Tiger Woods just before the Accenture Match Play Championship. Upon learning that he would be playing against Woods in the first round: "Anything can happen, especially where [Tiger's] hitting the ball."

- In August 2004, when asked what he liked about the Whistling Straits course, the site of the PGA Championship: "It's green. That's about all I'll say."

- In September 2004, when asked about being selected to play for the International team in the Presidents Cup: "When the time comes for me to play the Presidents Cup, then I'll decide if I'm going to play or not. I might be the first not to play."

- In July 2005, he was asked whether he felt a geographical divide in support, that Ames was Western Canada's guy and that Mike

Weir was Eastern Canada's: "Is he? Or is it Salt Lake's?" (Weir has lived in Utah for many years). "I don't know, you tell me?"

- On the condition of the Medinah golf course, the site of the PGA Championship in 2006: "Weak. Terrible. But you learn from these experiences. I don't know what I'll learn from this, but we'll see."

- When asked if the average fan in his adopted country recognizes him as Canadian: "No, never have. It's fine, doesn't bother me. That's their opinion, not mine."

There's no doubt that Stephen Ames shoots from the hip, but over the years his candid comments have sometimes overshadowed his success as a professional golfer. In his 12 years on the PGA circuit, Ames has won four titles, had top-10 finishes in three of the four majors and earned close to $18 million.

"I've always spoken my mind," said Ames. "It got me in trouble a couple of times, but I've dealt with it. The things I'm saying are not false statements, are they? But they are statements we are probably all thinking of."

The Stephen Ames story starts on the island nation of Trinidad and Tobago where he was born in 1964. Both his mother and father were also born in the Caribbean paradise, his father of English ancestry, his mother of Portuguese. His father was an executive for Texaco and spent much of his time away from home.

Ames, the eldest of four children (two boys, two girls) was part of the privileged white minority in a predominantly black country. He played golf at Pointe-à-Pierre Golf Club, which was mostly reserved for executives of large companies on the island. Golf was in his blood; his grandmother was a two-time Trinidad and Tobago amateur champion.

When he was 13, Ames became hooked on golf. As the son of a company employee, Ames lived in a compound that had facilities for tennis, soccer, basketball and other sports. And, of course, there was the golf course: "I lived about 70 yards from the fifth hole," he remembered.

As an amateur player, Ames dominated the local tournaments, winning the Caribbean Classic every year from age 16 until he was 22. He earned a golf scholarship to play at the College of Boca Raton in Florida and graduated with a business degree in 1985. In between semesters he played mini-tour events to improve his game.

He returned home from college to work for his father's successful maintenance company but lasted only 18 months. Golf, after all, was his passion; after work he would hit balls for two or three hours. Finally he told his father that he wanted to play professional golf, a plan his dad wasn't too happy about.

In 1987 at age 23, his father relented, staking him $5000 to get started. He finished 11th in the Jamaican Open, winning $1200, his first substantial payday. Ames made the jump to the U.S. mainland and played in several mini-tours, but he struggled at first and his money began to run out. Ames couldn't afford a car so he ended up taking the bus to each event.

In May 1989 his luck changed when he qualified to play on the Canadian Tour. He met his future wife, Jodi, a flight attendant from Calgary, while traveling to a tournament. "She was working business class but changed with her friend to work economy when she saw me back there," said Ames in an interview in ScoreGolf.com. "I asked her out for dinner when we landed, and she said yes."

Ames graduated to the Nationwide Tour (then called the Hogan Tour) in 1990 and was named rookie of the year. For the next three years, he played on the second-tier circuit, winning two

tournaments, but failing in his attempts to qualify for the PGA Tour.

He married Jodi in 1991 just as she was laid
off. His new wife ended up caddying for him for
the next two years on the Hogan Tour. In 1992,
he had an argument with a U.S. border guard
over his citizenship status (the guard said Ames
had claimed to be an American citizen;
Ames said he resided in the U.S.). He lost his
work visa and had to play on the European Tour
for the next six years. He won two events in
Europe against strong fields and averaged
$250,000 a year in purses.

But life on the road wore down the young
couple, and in 1994, they decided to settle down
in Calgary. Ames would play five weeks on the
road in Europe, come home for a couple of
weeks and then return to the European circuit.
In 1997, he finished an impressive fifth at the
British Open. Finally, a combination of help
from the PGA, various immigration lawyers and
saintly behaviour by Ames, resulted in the
restrictions being lifted.

Ames easily qualified for the PGA circuit in
1998 (the same year Weir joined the Tour), finishing tied for third at the PGA qualifying school
tournament. After a couple of learning seasons
in which he made enough money to keep his

playing card, Ames established himself as an up and comer with four top-10 finishes.

In 2002, he finished second at the Players Championship behind Craig Perks and made almost $1.3 million to jump to 46th in the world rankings. After another $1 million plus season in 2003 (he also became a Canadian citizen), Ames won his first PGA title at the Cialis Western Open.

"Having my family there meant so much," he said after winning $864,000 first place money. "It was perfect for everybody. But I don't think I'm too high. For me, the word is 'finally.' I've been waiting for this for a while. Sunday, it all came together—the whole week, actually. But I always knew it was there, inside me."

At the 2004 U.S. Open he finished ninth and again challenged at the PGA Championship with another ninth-place standing. Ames had joined Mike Weir to give Canada two legitimate PGA stars. He jumped up the world rankings into the top 20 (19th) and earned over $3.3 million (10th on the money list).

In 2005, golf took a back seat to family matters when his wife was diagnosed with lung cancer. After surgery in July to remove half of one lung, Jodi made a remarkable recovery. Two months later at the Canadian Open in Vancouver, she brought the couple's two sons to watch her husband play the final two rounds.

Thousands of other fans were following Ames at the Shaughnessy Golf and Country Club. The day before, Ames had shot a six-under-par 64 to move into contention. During the final round, he was within two shots of the leader Mark Calcavecchia before a double-bogey on the 13th ended his title hopes.

Ames ended up in seventh place, four shots behind Calcavecchia. He later admitted that the burden of his wife's illness had affected his play in the months leading up to the Canadian Open. "It was very difficult for me to focus or even see shots that I wanted to play because there were other things that were playing in my mind," said Ames. "It was difficult, very difficult."

"I've definitely felt a weight off my shoulders, the fact it's behind us now," he said about Jodi's rapid recovery. "All we can do now is go forward and try to stay healthy, like every family."

Ames was hoping for a comeback year in 2006. The season didn't start well when an off-hand comment about Tiger Woods' accuracy off the tee came back to haunt the free-speaking Canadian. When Ames said, "Anything can happen, especially where he's hitting the ball."

He claims he meant no slight against Woods, that instead it was a tribute to Tiger's ability to shoot great scores when he was in trouble.

At the Accenture Match Play Championship at La Costa, Ames was paired against Woods in the first round. Tiger birdied eight of the first nine holes to defeat Ames 9 and 8 (the largest amount a player can possibly lose by in an 18-hole match is 10 and 8). It was a slaughter from the outset, and Woods showed no mercy in humbling his opponent.

"What am I going to do, sit down and cry about it?" Ames said of the embarrassing loss. "He's the number one player in the world, and he played well for...was it nine or ten holes? That was it."

"We all know Stephen is a person who likes to speak his mind," said Woods later. "He's opinionated, and I think he's very honest. When he's asked a question, he answers it honestly, and I think that's what he did there—and it is what it is."

To his credit, Ames took his lumps and came back two months later to win the biggest title of his career at the Tournament Players Championship at Sawgrass. The TPC is referred to as the "fifth major" in the golf world, and Ames defeated the best players in the world to win his second PGA tournament.

Ames played the best final round of his life to overwhelm the field. He was able to pull away from everyone by shooting a five-under 67; he won by six shots over two-time U.S. Open champion Retief Goosen.

"It felt like a walk in the park, the way I was playing and putting," he admitted later.

Ames hit 72 percent of the greens and 75 percent of the fairways over the four days. It was precision golf at its finest. NBC golf analyst Johnny Miller said Ames won "...with old-time shot-making."

The victory at Sawgrass was worth $1.44 million (the largest cheque ever taken home by a Canadian player) and a five-year exemption in having to qualify for the Tour. "This is big," Ames said after finishing at 14-under par for the tourney. "This is characterized as the fifth major. I beat the top players in the world."

One of those players was Tiger Woods who finished 15 shots behind the leader. "That's golf," said Woods. "Each week is so different. Stephen didn't really play all that well when he played against me in the Match Play. The great thing about this game is it starts over the very next week."

By winning the TPC, Ames automatically received an invitation to play at the Masters two weeks later. A long-planned family vacation, however, stood in the way, and Ames told the world he wasn't sure he would accept the invitation because he "would rather go on a holiday to be honest."

Not surprisingly, Ames received a lot of flack for even considering turning down a chance to win the holy grail of golf. In the end, he cut the holiday down to a week and showed up at Augusta National with his family.

Ames said he never intended to spurn an invitation to the Masters, but that he needed to talk the matter over with his wife. "It was just a matter of letting her and the kids know their two weeks (planned vacation) would be cut short, that we wouldn't be going to Trinidad, and we were coming here to play golf," he said.

Playing in his second Masters (he had finished 45th the year before), Ames had a solid week, finishing tied for 11th spot. He would go on to finish the year earning almost $2.4 million (36th on the money list), his second best season on the Tour.

In 2007, Ames once again faced Tiger Woods, this time on a much bigger stage, the PGA Championship in Tulsa, Oklahoma. After shooting two straight rounds in the 60s, Ames was faced with a delicate 15-footer on the 18th to close out Saturday's third round. His reward for making the putt would be a final round pairing with Woods.

Ames took a long look at the leaderboard before striking the ball. The putt trickled toward the hole, caught the right-hand lip and went in. "I'm aggressively trying to get closer to him, that's what," said Ames when asked if he had considered the implications of sinking the putt. "He's got a three-shot lead, right? Five in front of him might not be enough, but three back is better than four."

Players often find that being in Tiger's company during the final round of a major is not much fun. In retrospect, Ames might have been better off missing the birdie putt the day before. Woods' fearsome presence in closing out tournaments has intimidated many a playing partner. Ames ended up shooting a six-over-par 76 to drop from second to a tie for 12th as Tiger rolled on to his 13th major title.

"I was fighting my swing, right off the start, and from there it was a struggle to get back into it," summed up Ames, who showed his nervousness by hitting his opening tee shot into the trees.

The 43-year-old Calgarian bogeyed four holes on the front side and then added four consecutive bogeys after the turn to complete his freefall down the standings. "I was fighting myself more than anything else," said Ames. "I wasn't fighting him, I was trying to play my game and trying to be me, and I couldn't be me today, unfortunately."

Two months later, Ames was back on his game, winning his third PGA tournament with a victory at the Children's Miracle Network Classic at Lake Buena Vista, Florida. In winning the $828,000 first-place cheque, Ames had to hold off the field with three birdies down the stretch. On the 18th, his second shot landed in a bunker. He was faced with a 65-foot sand shot, which he nailed within a few feet of the hole. A short putt later, and he had the par he needed to avoid a playoff.

"It was icing on the cake, the last event of the year," said Ames, who had made changes in his swing to hit the ball higher and straighter. "I was happy with the fact that I was coming down to the end and had to hit particular golf shots. The only one I'd like back, obviously, was the second one on 18. But this was a lot tougher that winning the TPC. There I had six shots [lead]. Here I had one."

Ames ended up finishing the year with $2.1 million in earnings (31st on money list) and raised his ranking to 33rd in the world. The only disappointment he suffered was his exclusion from the Presidents Cup team in September. International team captain Gary Player picked Weir over Ames for the match against the United States, even though Ames had a better world ranking and was the hotter player.

It was a double disappointment because the event was being held at the Royal Montreal Golf Club. Weir delighted the home crowd with a victory over Tiger Woods in a single's match on the final day. Ames never had that chance and was once again relegated to "the other Canadian" status.

"I was disappointed," admitted Ames. "I felt Gary could have picked both of us. I think both of us would have been a great attribute to the event itself and to the team, because the other guy he picked (Australia's Nick O'Hern) didn't play well at all."

With his revamped swing, Ames had a solid 2008 season. He made the cut in 19 of the 24 events he played, had seven top-10 finishes, won almost $2.3 million (27th on the money list) and improved his ranking to 27th in the world. At the age of 44, the slim Calgarian had his most consistent year on the Tour.

In 2009, Ames saved a so-so season by winning the Children's Miracle Network Classic for a second time, defeating George McNeill and Justin Leonard on the second extra hole of a playoff. It was the first time in 291 starts on the PGA Tour that Ames had been in a playoff. The victory, worth $846,000, vaulted him to 37th on the money list with earnings of $2.1 million.

Heading into the 2010 season, the irony of Stephen Ames is that a strong case can be made that he is our most authentic Canadian golfer. Even though Ames was born and raised in Trinidad and Tobago, he has lived in Calgary for over a decade and has become a Canadian citizen. Mike Weir, our most celebrated golfer, has long resided in Salt Lake City, Utah.

In choosing to come to Canada, Ames has given golf fans in his adopted country the treat of watching two elite players thrive at the highest level of the sport.

Chapter Four

Lorie Kane
The Late Bloomer

Born Charlottetown, PEI, 1964–

Lorie Kane's path to stardom on the LPGA Tour did not follow the blueprint set out for most young women aspiring to become professional golfers. First of all, Kane hails from Prince Edward Island, hardly a hotbed for female pro golfers. Then she resisted heading south on a golf scholarship; instead she pursued her university studies in Canada. Finally, she waited a long time to give up her amateur status, turning pro at age 29 and beginning her LPGA career two years later.

In the end, however, it all worked for Kane. In 14 seasons on the LPGA circuit she has won four times, in the process becoming the all-time earnings leader in Canadian female golfer history, notching over $6.7 million (15th in LPGA career earnings).

In 2000, she had one of the most remarkable years of any Canadian golfer. After finishing second nine times in her first three years on the Tour, Kane broke through with three LPGA titles during the 2000 campaign. She earned $929,189 over the season, shattering the Canadian record for LPGA earnings in a year, and finished fifth on the LPGA money list.

Lorie Kane began playing golf at the age of five. Her father, Jack, was the first coach to take the young girl under his wing and teach her how to play the game like a professional. A top local amateur player, Jack was the Canadian Professional Golf Association's head pro at Brudenell River Golf Course in Montague, PEI. Later, he worked at the Belvedere Golf Club in Charlottetown, where, Lorie, then 11, took lessons while working at the club. An island legend, Cec Dowling was the head pro at Belvedere and helped Kane develop the elegant and smooth swing that became her trademark.

At one time in her teenage years, she was known as a better basketball player than golfer. She played on the same high school hoops team as her sister Mary-Lynn. Her prep coach Dave

MacNeil became a mentor, encouraging Kane to work hard to reach her athletic potential. When MacNeil took a varsity coaching job at the University of Prince Edward Island, he recruited Lorie to join his basketball team. She played in PEI for one year, before transferring to Acadia University in Wolfville, Nova Scotia.

Besides basketball, Kane was also a decent synchronized swimmer. She said that playing other sports was invaluable experience for what lay ahead on the golf course. "I'm lucky to have played other sports," she said in a 1998 profile in *Maclean's* magazine. "I mean, in basketball, you never died, never gave up."

In 1982, she won her first golf tournament, the PEI junior championship, and over the next decade she added nine provincial ladies' amateur titles. By 1989, she had begun representing Canada at international tournaments, including being a member of the Canadian Commonwealth Team in 1991.

In 1992, Kane expected to wear the Maple Leaf again, this time as a member of the Canadian contingent at the World Amateur Championship. Kane was told by the Canadian Ladies Golf Association that the criteria for making the team had changed and that she had not qualified. Kane thought the decision unjust and took her case to court in PEI. The CLGA applied for a stay of order, which was refused, so amid considerable tension, Kane was included on the team. The event was held in Vancouver and for the young woman from PEI who always got along with everyone, it was a lesson in toughening up and developing a thick skin.

"That experience [at Marine Drive in Vancouver] was real difficult for me," said Kane. "I learned a lot about who I was and how to deal with things. The three-wood I hit off the first tee at Marine Drive the first day was the most pressure I have ever felt. I felt more pressure on that tee than playing the back nine on tour knowing I have the lead."

In 1989, she also hooked up with legendary Canadian coach Jack McLaughlin. For several months she lived with the McLaughlin family in Vancouver, working on her golf game, and just as importantly, receiving encouragement from McLaughlin that she could succeed as a professional golfer.

At the age of 29, Kane turned pro and began playing the du Maurier Series, a five-event tour she won in 1994 and 1995. While playing on the Central Florida Challenge Tour, another developmental series mini-tour, she met Danny Sharp, a former pro golfer, who had competed on the Canadian Tour and in South America.

Sharp was recovering from a serious car accident that had ended his pro career. While watching Kane on the driving range, he offered to give her some tips to improve her game. The two became good friends, and Kane asked Sharp to be her full-time caddie. Sharp grew to understand Kane's game and advised her when to take risks and when to play it safe.

"It's important for her just to get herself ready to play each shot," explained the Hamilton native. "I take care of the rest."

In 1995, Kane tied for 48th at the LPGA Final Qualifying Tournament to earn non-exempt status (a provisional standing allowing her to compete for a spot that has come open due to a withdrawal on the Monday before each tournament) for the 1996 season. She managed to qualify for nine events and made the cut in four of them, including an eighth place finish at one stop in Boston. Kane returned to the qualifying tournament at the end of the year and finished third to earn a full-time spot for the 1997 LPGA season.

At the age of 31, she was finally ready to tackle the LPGA circuit. She had a supportive network of friends and family in place, including Sharp, McNeil and her eldest sister Mary-Lynn Jenkins, a lawyer, took care of the business side.

She had an amazing coming-out party. She played 30 events in 1997 and made the cut in 28 of them. She was in the top 10 eight times, including four, second-place finishes; Toray Japan Queens Cup, the Susan G. Komen International, State Farm Rail Classic (where she lost to Cindy Figg-Currier in a sudden-death playoff) and the ITT LPGA Tour Championship (another playoff loss, this time to Annika Sorenstam).

"At the beginning of year, I just wanted to make the cut," said Kane midway through the season. "That's not even in the back of my mind now. Now I ask myself what I have to do to win, to be in a position to win."

In her first full season she earned $425,964 to finish 11th on the money list. She had quickly become one of the tour's top players and developed a reputation as one of its most likeable. Kane garnered attention for her golf game and the way she conducted herself on the course. She stood out for the almost constant smile and easy-going demeanor. She quietly became the new envoy of women's golf in Canada, a role she was willing to take on.

"I'm quite honoured with that," said Kane. "If I'm going to be recognized as a happy, smiling Canadian, I am more than happy to assume that role. I'm excited to be in the position I'm in. If it helps the rest of the Canadians make it on to the tour, I'll gladly drag them right along with me."

There was no sophomore jinx in 1998. She made the cut in 29 of 32 events and added 12 more top-10 finishes. Her best result was a second place tie at the Chick-fil-A Charity Championship. She won $508,249 to place 12th on the money list.

"I've just tried to keep on a roll," said Kane about her busy schedule that included playing in more events than any other LPGA player. "I played a lot of golf last year, and I played even more this year. I haven't taken much time off, but it's taken me a little time to get here [on tour], and I'm trying to make up for lost time."

Kane also became a full-blown celebrity on Prince Edward Island. A trip home almost became more exhausting than the rigors of the LPGA circuit as she accepted congratulations from family and friends and contended with countless requests from the local media. For the first time she really began to feel the pressure to win her first LPGA title.

In 1999, she came close three more times. She would finish second at the Standard Register PING and then suffer two more playoff defeats—a first hole sudden-death loss to Rachel Hetherington at the Chick-fil-A Charity event and a heart-breaking fifth extra hole loss to Sherri Steinhauer at the Japan Airlines Big Apple Classic.

Despite missing the winner's circle, Kane crafted a wonderful season that included 13 top-10 results. She made the cut an amazing 29 times in 30 events, finishing with $757,844 to place fifth on the money list.

With nine runner-up finishes on her résumé, golfing pundits began to openly question whether Kane had the mental fortitude to win an LPGA event. "When the tournaments and the playoffs are over, it's done," explained the frustrated islander. "You guys in the media do a good job of reminding us about this, and it's good that you do that."

"I know it's in my future. The only pressure I feel is what's put on me from outside things: the media, the fans. All we can do is go out and play our best."

In her preparation for the next season, Kane's goal was to establish as much control as possible every week. "I came out in January wanting to win a golf tournament, and I had a pretty good run at it in our first event," said Kane about the start of the 2000 campaign. "I played well in Australia, and then I had a bad round at the Dinah Shore. I felt things were falling apart, which wasn't the case."

After feeling unhappy about her game for a couple of months and then having her golf clubs go missing on a flight, Kane decided to take a week off. She asked her old high school basketball coach Dave MacNeil to visit her in Florida. He spent three days with her, trying to rid his former hoop player of the self-doubt that had crept into her game when under pressure.

In August at the Michelob Light Classic, Kane had again put herself in contention to win a title. She had the lead heading into the final round, and deep down the Charlottetown native knew that she could win the title.

"The forecast was for bad weather, and they put a note up in the locker room saying there was chance for flooding," she told the media a few days after the tournament ended. "Part of me was saying if we didn't play, I'd win. But I knew if we did play, I would win anyway. I wanted to play. I felt very different, more relaxed and confident."

She ended up playing the final day and winning by three strokes. In the enthusiastic gallery waiting to celebrate her victory on the 18th hole was a large contingent of fellow pros that ringed the putting surface in anticipation of her first LPGA win. When Kane sank the putt, her peers welcomed her into the winner's club by dousing her with beer.

"For some of those girls to change plane tickets and reservations to stay with me and to celebrate with me really meant a lot," said Kane, reflecting on the victory. "The beer shower was a lot of fun. I don't think I've worn that outfit since. I don't know if I ever will."

The victory took a huge burden off Kane's golf game. "There were times, at different points, where I would just wish people wouldn't say to me, 'When are you going to win?' because I was trying to do everything I could. I think as a result I put too much pressure on myself."

"Now looking back, I'm glad I finished second nine times. I'm glad I didn't win the playoffs in 1997 at the Tour Championships with Annika Sorenstam and Pat Hurst because I don't think I was ready to win then. I think I needed to build a foundation, a solid foundation of what I have now. And I think I would never have had that opportunity had I won right off the bat."

Her success continued through the late stages of the 2000 season. She won both the New Albany Golf Classic and the Mizuno Open (a birdie on the first playoff hole). In a 10-week run, she won three times and finished in the top 10 in eight events. In December, she was named Canada's female athlete of the year (she had also won the award after the 1997 season).

"I got off to a good start then kind of hit the skids," summed up Kane on her up and down season. "For some reason, in August I really turned things around and started playing some great golf."

Heading into the 2001 season, the stakes were even higher. Kane was now ranked as one of the LPGA's best players, and the expectation was that she needed to add a major title to her golfing record to be considered a great golfer. She was a model of consistency—26 cuts made in 27 events; 14 top 10s, including her fourth Tour victory at the LPGA Takefuji Classic where she shot a final round 63 to hold off a hard charging Sorenstam. Kane finished the season earning $947,489, fourth on the money list.

It was a year when a trio of players—Sorenstam, Se Ri Pak and Karrie Webb—had separated themselves from the rest of the LPGA pack; all three had earned more than $1.5 million. Sorenstam had won eight times and earned over $2.1 million, setting a new benchmark for female pros.

Kane admitted she wasn't in their league, but sent out mixed messages on whether she was committed to catching them. "My goal has been to be the best player out here," said Kane. "Annika's year has been spectacular. I think I can challenge that."

Kane decided that she needed to devote more time to physical conditioning to take the next step. But her very nature was at odds with what would be required to catch the Swedish superstar.

"I think the mechanics of my swing are fine anyway," she said, admitting that she doesn't enjoy hitting balls for hours on the range. "I think I have what it takes there. Besides, I like to give myself time just to be Lorie. I like being with my family, with being home. I respect Annika a great deal for what she's done, and I have to ask myself if I can do what she does, if I can commit myself to being where she is. I have to decide if I want to be the No. 1 player or if it's enough to challenge every week."

One of Kane's goals was to win the du Maurier Championship on home soil. She was a contender in 1999 (6th-place tie) and 2000 (5th-place tie) but was never able to provide her hometown fans with a victory. Her record in the other women's major championships was also disappointing. A fourth place finish in the 1999 U.S. Open is her best result.

For the next four seasons, Kane continued playing at a high level, earning over $500,000 each year with 35 top-10 finishes. For nine straight seasons she was ranked no lower than 21st on the money list.

In 2006 her performance started to drop off. She had only a pair of top 10s in 28 events and fell to 42nd on the money list ($307,301). Two years later she only made the cut in nine of 22 events; her best finish was a tie for 31st.

As Kane's golfing career reaches the end of the line, she will be remembered for her consistency and durability over a 10-year stretch that began in 1997. In that time she stood out from a bevy of grim-faced women who seemed to be toiling over their work. It was never that way for Kane. Sportswriters have said she doesn't just "smile" on the course, but that she "beams." For the late starter, playing on the LPGA has been like winning the lottery each week.

"I get to travel the world, and I'm growing as a player and a person, with every new tournament we play and every new city we visit," she said early in her pro career. "I love it."

Chapter Five

Nelford and Leggatt
Promise Unfulfilled

Nelford: Born Vancouver, BC, 1955–
Leggatt: Born Cambridge, ON, 1965–

Even though Jim Nelford ended his abbreviated PGA journey two years before Ian Leggatt began as a Tour rookie, both Canadian players can be linked together by the old sporting cliché: "what might have been...." Injuries derailed them both just as they were reaching their peak competitive years.

Both came back from their physical ailments and tried to regain their standing on the Tour. Nelford failed, and though Leggatt is still hoping for a comeback on the Nationwide Tour, it looks as if his attempt will also fall short. Both are charismatic guys with a sense of humour. Neither is frightened to offer an opinion and tell it like it is. Nelford has used those tools to forge a successful commentating career as a TV golf analyst; Leggatt has been approached to take a spot in the television booth when he's finished playing.

Jim Nelford

In the book *Seasons in a Golfer's Life*, Nelford and writer Lorne Rubenstein teamed up to chronicle the British Columbian's rise to the PGA Tour. He grew up in the Vancouver-area and began playing golf seriously at age 13 when his father bought him a membership to the Pitt Meadows Golf Club. Before long he was breaking 80.

Mostly self-taught, Nelford progressed up the golfing ladder. In Grade 12, he won the BC High School Junior title, and later in 1973, he added the BC Junior championship. Through a family friend, Nelford auditioned for Karl Tucker, the golf coach at Brigham Young University in Provo, Utah.

In January 1974, he was offered a half scholarship to play golf at Brigham Young University, which he gladly accepted. As a freshman, Nelford was left off the first team and didn't play in any collegiate competitions. Back at home over the summer he was determined to return to school and make the team in 1975.

The next season was the turning point in Nelford's amateur career. He became a permanent team member at BYU, and then in 1975, he won the BC Amateur championship and the Canadian Amateur title. With five players tied for the lead with five holes left to play, Nelford eagled 15 and 16 to win the title by four shots.

"The win was huge," said Nelford years later, "especially making a major, major charge in the last few holes. It was magical, a real special moment."

Full of confidence, he won two NCAA tournaments for BYU in 1976. Nelford was part of a powerhouse program that would later send all six members of the team to the PGA Tour. By the end of the season, BYU had won seven straight events and finished second in the NCAA tournament.

Nelford defended his Canadian Amateur title in Victoria by going five under on the last 10 holes to tie for the lead. On the second play-off hole, Nelford birdied to beat Mexico's Rafael Alarcon. By this time, the left-hander was recognized as Canada's next great golfing hope.

In 1977, Nelford's last college year, he was a second-team All-American. Still an amateur, he played the Canadian Open at Glen Abbey for the first time and made the cut. A week later he won the prestigious Western Amateur in Michigan by defeating Alarcon in the final match. Next came the Canadian Amateur in Hamilton. Nelford had a seven-shot lead after the first two rounds. But the effects of playing so much golf in a short period of time finally caught up with him, and he finished with a 75–73 to place second, two shots behind Rod Spittle.

In November, Nelford was one of 144 players going for 30 spots on the PGA Tour at the qualifying school in Pinehurst. In the first three rounds, he shot 74-72-76 to stand in 13th place. After a shaky double-bogey, bogey start, Nelford birdied three of the next five holes. He ended up shooting a final round 73 to easily earn his PGA Tour card.

As a PGA rookie, Nelford finished in the top 10 in three tournaments, including third-place ties at the Tallahassee and Southern Open events. He would earn just under $30,000, good enough for 87th on the money list.

In the early parts of 1979, Nelford had two top-15 results on the West Coast. Never a great driver of the ball, instead relying on his iron play and putting to score, Nelford decided to swing harder off the tee. Unfortunately, he tore the muscles in his left shoulder from the increased pressure of his swing.

Nelford was still in pain when he finished eighth at the Canadian Open in June. He struggled through the rest of the year, missing the cut in five of his last 11 tournaments. He finished with just over $40,000 in total earnings, dropping to 95th on the money list.

In 1980, Nelford continued to struggle on the PGA circuit. The one bright spot came in December after the Tour had ended, when he and Dan Halldorson represented Canada at the World Cup in Bogota, Columbia. The two combined to open up a seven-shot lead on Scotland after three rounds. The nervous Canadian pair saw their lead drop to two shots by the 13th hole. On the 14th, Scotland's Sandy Lyle eagled to pull dead even with Canada.

Nelford and Halldorson pulled away from the Scottish pair once again and held a two-shot advantage at the 18th tee. Nelford's approach shot on the final hole landed 15 feet from the cup, putting more pressure on Scotland to come up with a pair of miracle shots. When both Lyle and his playing partner Steve Martin failed in their birdie attempts; Nelford was left with an easy two-putt for the World Cup.

Nelford summed up the importance of the win in his book: "I had had fun playing most of my life until I got into my second year on Tour. Now, after my last two disappointing seasons, I wanted to look over a shot and feel good. After the World Cup, I at least felt eager again."

The 1981 season was a wash out. Nelford made a little over $20,000 to finish 132nd on the money list. He only made the cut in 14 of 30 tournaments. By 1982, Nelford's shoulder was fully healed, and he began to make slight gains in the quality of his game. Early in the season, he finished seventh at the L.A. Open. After a mid-season slump, he again finished seventh at the Kemper Open to win $12,050, his biggest payday on the Tour. The result lifted his earnings over $30,000, guaranteeing Nelford a place in the top 125 on the money list and a full exemption the following year.

Without the burden of qualifying for each tournament, Nelford had the breakout season many golf observers had predicted years earlier. He was in contention at the Crosby National Pro-Am until a final round 75 knocked him down to 14th place. The result was still worth $19,000. At the Heritage Classic, Nelford trailed Fuzzy Zoeller by only two shots after 54 holes. Playing in the final group with Zoeller, the now battle-tested Canadian held the lead after 10 holes.

A bogey on the 15th, followed by a double-bogey on the 16th, cost Nelford a chance of beating Zoeller, but the second-place finish and the $37,600 cheque was a definite confidence booster. He ended up winning $112,000 in total prize money in 1982, missing the cut in only five of the 31 events. Nelford's total earnings placed him 50th on the money list.

In 1984, Nelford placed himself in even better position to win his first PGA event. At the Bing Crosby National Pro-Am at Pebble Beach he was the leader in the clubhouse with a one-stroke lead over Hale Irwin. On the par-5 18th, Irwin snap-hooked his drive into Carmel Bay, only to have it bounce off a rock back into the fairway.

"It was probably the luckiest break a golfer's ever gotten," said Nelford many years later in an interview with *Sports Illustrated*. Needing a birdie to force a playoff, Irwin hit a third-shot wedge onto the green. The ball took one hop, hit the flagstick and stopped five feet from the cup. Irwin sank the putt to force a playoff.

On the second hole of the sudden-death playoff, Irwin made another remarkable shot when it seemed Nelford had the advantage. After sending his drive into a bunker with 210 yards to reach the green, Irwin hit an iron within a few feet of the hole and sank his putt for a birdie and the victory.

This time Nelford didn't make any glaring mistakes to take himself out of contention; it took top-notch shot making and lot of luck for Irwin to prevail at Pebble Beach. At the age of 29, Nelford seemed poised to become a PGA star.

His golfing career was suddenly ambushed just over a year later. In July 1985, Nelford was nearly killed in a water skiing accident on Saguaro Lake near his home in Phoenix. He had finished a run and was treading water when the boat that had been pulling him suddenly came back towards him. Nelford had just enough time to avoid a direct hit, but the boat's propeller blade tore into his right arm between the hand and elbow.

"My last thought was, 'Get to one side of the boat or you're dead.' I should have been shredded."

Nelford was unconscious when he arrived at the hospital in Phoenix. Doctors wanted to amputate his arm, but his mother explained that Nelford was a professional golfer and asked that they try to save it. The medical team put 13 screws in the arm and spent hours reattaching tendons, cartilage and nerves.

After a nine-day stay at the hospital, Nelford began the long process of healing and rehabbing his arm. He played his first PGA event 11 months after the accident, shooting a 79 at the Gerry Ford Invitational. He played three PGA events in all in 1986 but failed to make the cut in any of them.

"After the accident, I had no idea what the mental and emotional challenges would be," said Nelford. "I thought the physical challenges would be enormous, and they were, but the mental and emotional challenges were off the charts."

In 1987, the PGA allowed him to play in any tournament he wanted to enter, but with only two-thirds use of his right arm, he was required to make swing and grip changes that restricted his shot-making ability. At the end of the season, he was forced back to qualifying school just to keep his playing card.

Over six grueling rounds Nelford put his new golf game to the ultimate test. Amazingly, he played solid golf over all six days, shooting a final round even par 72 to place sixth and easily retain his card.

"A lot of times I lay in bed and wondered if I'd ever be able to play golf at this level again," he said after it was over. "It's nice to get through a tournament like this because it's not a fun one to play."

Unfortunately, Nelford couldn't build any momentum off his qualifying school success. In 1988 he only earned $20,000 to finish 200th on the money list, well short of the top 125 needed to keep his card. He again had to tackle Q-school, but this time he wasn't able to regain his card.

In 1991, he abandoned his dreams of playing on the PGA circuit to become a golf commentator for ESPN. With his full head of dark hair, handsome features and the ability to provide terse and incisive commentary, Nelford quickly established a reputation as a top-notch analyst.

In 1994, CBS hired Nelford to work the World Series of Golf, the Presidents Cup, the Masters and the PGA championship. The next year, the Golf Channel made him their chief analyst at men's tournaments. He continued to work as a broadcaster right up to 2007 when his contract with the U.S. network ran out.

Through his years as a broadcaster he still craved to play at the top level. "I miss so much of what I had," summed up Nelford. "There's nothing like the feeling of walking down the last few fairways with a chance to win."

━ ━

Ian Leggatt

Ian Leggatt started golfing at age nine, riding his bike to a club in Cambridge, Ontario about two kilometres from his house.

Hockey, like most Canadian boys, was Leggatt's passion, and he played regularly until the age of 12. Along the way he took up speed skating as a way to strengthen his legs winning several regional speed skating titles as a teenager and was even a member of the Canadian indoor team.

"Somehow or other, I was really good at it," remembers Leggatt. "I was on the junior national team, and as a kid, it's fun winning trophies. In speed skating, there's a competition every weekend, so I was winning a trophy every week rather than waiting until the end of the year to collect."

At 18, Leggatt quit skating to concentrate on golf. He made the World Cup team as an amateur and earned a golf scholarship at Tex Wesleyan, which is a small American university that has attracted a number of Canadian players over the years. He became a NAIA All-American and earned a degree in sports management.

After graduating in 1990, he took a job as the athletic director of the United Cerebral Palsy Foundation in Fort Worth, a position that paid just $15,000 a year. A professional golf career was the last thing on his mind until he asked a former university sponsor about helping out with an overnight camp for kids. The man asked why Leggatt wasn't playing professional golf and offered to sponsor him.

Over the next nine years, Leggatt became a golfing nomad. After easily qualifying to play on the Canadian Tour, he juggled a schedule that also included trips to Australia, Asia, South Africa and South America. In all those years, he played well enough to support himself but never managed a big win. On the Canadian Tour, he had finished second six times—an agonizing string of close calls. Then came a number of unsuccessful attempts at getting through PGA qualifying school.

In 2000, Leggatt realized he was treading water and decided to take the plunge by playing the Buy.com Tour with the goal of qualifying for the PGA. By making a minor adjustment in his hand position, the 33-year-old was able to overcome the last hurdle in his development as a consistent player—improved putting—to take a run at earning his PGA card.

He had two runner-up finishes in the early part of the season, then in June he two-putted for a birdie in a playoff at the Dayton Open to win his first professional victory. The $76,500 top prize guaranteed Leggatt a top-15 finish on the Buy.com money list and a full PGA Tour exemption the next year.

"Getting away from Canada has helped me focus on getting my PGA card," summed up Leggatt. "The Canadian Tour is a good developmental tour, but a lot of Canadians become too comfortable playing at home. I think I fell into that rut for a while. After a while, you should start to hate it and try to get to the next level."

Leggatt ended up finishing fifth on the money list. He discovered that as a powerful, long hitter, his game was perfectly suited to the mega-sized championship-style courses played on both the Buy.com and PGA tours. Leggatt had also gained a quiet confidence by playing in tournaments all over the world.

"Although every year you enter Tour school hoping to get there, maybe in the back of my mind I knew I wasn't ready to go out there and feel like I could succeed," he explained. "But now I really do, I feel like I'm ready. Everything comes in due time, and I think my learning process or belief in myself has taken a little longer than some other people. I really feel like now my game is ready and I'm personally ready so I'm looking forward to it."

Leggatt started slowly in his first year competing against the best players in the world. The Tour rookie had laser eye surgery before he reached the PGA circuit, but as the season progressed he realized his sight had regressed.

After missing eight straight cuts, he went for another round of surgery. Once recovered, he earned cheques in 11 of his next 14 events, including consecutive top-10 finishes at the John Deere Classic and Buick Open. After adding an 18th-place finish at the Canadian Open it seemed certain that Leggatt would keep his card.

Needing just a couple of solid results in the last few tournaments, his vision began to blur again. This time Leggatt decided to delay another surgery and slumped badly at the wrong time. He finished the year with $368,862 in earnings, but that was only good enough for 133rd on the money list (the top 125 keep their cards).

After getting his eye touched up once again, Leggatt tied for fifth at the qualifying school to earn his way back to the Tour in 2002. In February, competing in the middle of the desert in Arizona, Leggatt shot a final round eight-under-par 64 to win the Tucson Open by two shots to capture his first PGA title.

Leggatt charged up the leaderboard on the final day, passing 15 players who began the round with equal or better scores. On the 17th hole, Leggatt chipped to within five feet and sank the birdie putt to open up his two-shot lead. After a perfect drive on the final hole, Leggatt hit his approach shot into a bunker just above the hole and was faced with a tricky sand shot. Without pondering over the shot, Leggatt blasted out of the sand to within 10 inches from the cup.

The victory was worth $540,000 and a two-year exemption on the Tour, an important perk for the 36-year-old who had always had to struggle to maintain his place in golf's pecking order.

The win also came with a bit of irony. Normally when a Canadian golfer wins a PGA title, it becomes front-page news in the sports section at home. Leggatt's victory was completely overshadowed by the men's Olympic gold medal hockey game in Salt Lake City. An on-course reporter from the Golf Channel was giving Leggatt updates on the game. On the long walk between the 17th green and the 18th tee, the reporter whispered the words: "Canada 5, the United States 2. Less than a minute to go."

With the news, Leggatt stung his drive down the middle of the fairway and made par on the toughest hole of the course to secure the victory. "Getting it in the fairway on 18 was a double victory, I guess," said Leggatt later. "First time in 50 years Canada wins a gold medal, and I win my golf tournament. It was pretty awesome day."

"Now I can be a little more prepared and pick and choose the golf courses that I feel like I can be the best on," he said about earning the two-year PGA exemption. "That's how guys do it out here. A guy like Mike Weir is going to pick the weeks where he really enjoys to play."

The win in Tucson also qualified Leggatt to play in his first major tournament, the U.S. Open. He finished a very credible 20th, but injured his hand hitting out of the rough at the Black Course at Bethgate, New York. It would be the start of a string of hand injuries and other physical ailments that would all but end his career.

Leggatt finished the 2002 season with more than $1.2 million in total earnings—47th on the money list and 31 spots ahead of countryman Mike Weir. He was labelled a real up and comer until his body started to betray his potential as a solid PGA player.

Not only was the hand slow to heal, Leggatt was also told he was allergic to certain trees, grasses and pollens. He also suffered from painful tendonitis in his left elbow, an offshoot of a blood-circulation disorder in his thumb.

Worst of all he "felt tired, crappy all the time." He found out that he was suffering from Epstein-Barr virus (EBV is a member of the herpes virus family and one of the most common human viruses), which was sapping his energy at an alarming rate.

"From the research I've done on it since I was diagnosed, I found out that 75% of people are carrying this virus. It lies dormant in most instances, but in my case it came out," said Leggatt. "And when you're struggling with your health, trying to compensate for the way you feel, you fall into more and more bad habits with your game."

In 2003 he made the cut in only 11 of the 26 tournaments he entered. He began taking supplements to combat the effects of Epstein-Barr and eliminated bread products from his diet. A move from the dryness of Arizona to the dampness of North Carolina helped his allergies and relieved the bad sinus infections he had developed.

More challenges faced Leggatt in 2004. Just as he was starting to find his game again, his left wrist began to hurt. He was forced to shut things down by April to have two surgeries to relieve symptoms of carpal tunnel syndrome.

He ended up playing sparingly in both the 2004 and 2005 seasons and was granted a major medical exemption by the PGA Tour. He would need yet another round of surgery to clean up a bone spur around his wrist. "It's become a common thing; surgeries are like colds," summed up a dejected Leggatt.

Not wanting to be seen as a player that was taking advantage of his medical exemption, Leggatt ended up returning to the golf course before his hand had completely healed. In 2004, he went to Australia, and after playing in a couple of tournaments, was forced to endure yet another procedure. The next year, Leggatt needed more time to strengthen his hand and wrist and so postponed returning to the PGA Tour.

After the medical exemptions had run out, Leggatt qualified for the 2006 PGA season by finishing 18th at Q-school. He missed the cut in all but three of his first 17 tournaments, and even though he cashed cheques in seven of his final 12 events, it was not enough to keep him on the Tour.

Another run at Q-school ended in failure, and Leggatt was forced into playing a scrambled schedule of PGA and Nationwide events. In 2007, he missed the cut in each of the first 10 tournaments he played, and at the age of 41, was forced to consider his options.

"I don't feel I've done what I could have so far. I'd like to get one more (title)," he said. "I told my wife not long ago, if I got my game back in shape and won again, I could quit. That would be okay with me."

Leggatt has continued his comeback attempt on the Nationwide Tour for the last three years, and while making the cut in some events, he has been unable to recapture the game that propelled him to a PGA Tour win in 2002.

Chapter Six

The Girls from BC

In the 1990s, four young women from British Columbia found success on the LPGA Tour. All four, Dawn Coe-Jones, Lisa Walters, Gail Graham and Jennifer Wyatt won titles on the women's circuit. In all they combined to record nine LPGA victories in the decade. Three of the four—Coe-Jones, Walters and Graham—were eventually elected to the Canadian Golf Hall of Fame.

The BC contingent were beneficiaries of Title IX, a landmark 1972 American educational amendment banning sex discrimination in school, whether it be in academics or athletics.

The amendment meant that American universities had to offer an equal number of scholarships to female athletes. Previously, 90 percent of scholarships went to males. In the 1980s, American universities began offering Canadian women full-ride scholarships to play for their golf teams.

As a result of better competition and a longer golf season, Canadian players began to make a big impact on the LPGA circuit in the 1990s.

The first victories for the BC women came at the start of the 1992 LPGA season when Coe (she later became Dawn Coe-Jones when she married in 1993) pulled off an amazing double play for Canadian professional golfers. The week before, her roommate, Lisa Walters, won the Itoki Hawaiian Ladies Open, and Coe followed up with the duet on the island as she took home the Women's Kemper Open.

"It was spectacular, really storybook," said Coe about her first victory on the LPGA Tour after nine years on the circuit. "You'd have a better chance of winning the lottery than having the two of us win one week after another."

Coe was there to congratulate Walters, who at age 32 and after nine years on the circuit, had surprised golfing pundits by winning her first tournament. Walters apologized to her close friend, telling her that she should been the first of the pair to win a title. Coe replied that Walters should enjoy the win, and that her own time would come.

In the final round of the Kemper, the 31-year-old from Lake Cowichan, wired a birdie putt from

30 feet on the 15th, then came back with a second birdie by holing in from the fringe on the 16th. That put Coe in front to stay, as she finished off the round with two consecutive pars to win the tournament by a single shot over Dottie Mochrie.

Walters had also needed to score low in the final round to win her first title the week before. "I made four birdies in the first five holes," said Walters, a native of Prince Rupert, BC. "Since I started the round five shots from the lead I knew I was close. But I didn't worry, even though I was nervous for the middle six holes."

In the first two rounds, Walters shot a 71 and 72, and then came the birdies on the front nine that put her in contention. She didn't look at the leaderboard for the entire last round, and when she made it to the clubhouse with a two-stroke lead, Walters was shocked. Fortunately, the leaders faltered on the final holes, and Walters had her first LPGA Tour win.

"I went through a lot of problems in the last two years," explained Walters, who besides earning $60,000 also gained a much-coveted five-year qualifying exemption. "But I kept trying. Four years is a long time to be in a slump, but as long as I was making a little profit I was going to stay out."

And while Walters' win was an unexpected surprise, big things had been expected from her roommate. Dawn Coe had become Canada's best female golfer since Sandra Post retired in the mid-1980s. The thing missing on her golfing résumé was a title, which was finally rectified with the victory in Hawaii.

━ ━

Dawn Coe-Jones

Dawn Coe started playing golf at age nine, in her hometown of Lake Cowichan. Her father, a logger, was a good player, and his daughter had lots of time on the course to improve her game. A versatile athlete (she played guard on the Lake Cowichan Secondary Lakers Basketball Team, winners of the provincial championship in 1977), Coe won her first golf event at age 10.

By the age of 12, Coe began to break 80 and for the first time beat her father at a club tournament. She was rewarded with a new set of golf clubs and the opportunity to play in regional tournaments. Coe was a shy youngster and travelling away from home was hard, but luckily she had her mother on the road with her to ease her anxiety.

At the age of 18, she left Vancouver Island to play in her first provincial junior championship and won. She was also champion at her first national event, winning the 1978 Canadian junior nationals at Fredericton, New Brunswick.

In 1979, she defended her provincial junior title and finished fourth at the junior nationals. After high school, she nearly turned her back on pursuing a golf career but decided to try for a scholarship at Lamar University in Beaumont, Texas. A couple of other BC golfers (Graham and Wyatt) also ended up attending Lamar. The school was small, which made the transition to living away from home much easier for the still shy teenager, and the golf program was known for producing many talented professionals.

In her final year at Lamar in 1983, Coe was named a first-team All-American and won the Canadian Amateur championship. Brimming with confidence, she qualified for the LPGA Tour on her first try. She steadily improved her consistency on the pro circuit, winning more money each year except for 1988, after her mother's death, and 1991, when her father passed away. Both parents had been instrumental in her development as a golfer—her father was her first coach, her mother provided the emotional support required for the introverted youngster to keep accepting new challenges. In 1990, she earned nearly $290,000 to finish 11th on the LPGA money list. The next year, she won the Seoul Ladies Open in Korea, a non-LPGA event. Coe had become Canada's best female golfer, but it still took nine long

years for her to win her first LPGA title at the
Kemper Open in 1992.

"When I first came on the tour, I had no more
idea about winning than flying to the moon," said
Coe, who became recognizable to Canadian fans
with her trademark blond hair spilling over her
visor. "It was just making the cut, making
a cheque."

In 1993, she married Tampa, Florida, business-
man Jimmy Jones and became Dawn Coe-Jones.
She finished third at the du Maurier Classic that
year and then followed up with wins at the 1994
LPGA Palm Beach Classic and the 1995 Tournament of Champions. Coe-Jones became the first
Canadian woman to top $1 million in career
earnings.

At the first tournament of the season, the
Tournament of Champions in Florida, Coe-Jones
beat an elite field of 38 by shooting a seven-
under-par 281 in the 72-hole event. Her margin
of victory was six shots, and she earned $115,000,
a huge payday on the women's circuit.

Coe-Jones had moved to Florida three years
previously and had been able to play more in
the off-season. The extra practice allowed her to
get a quick start at the beginning of the year.
All three of her LPGA victories came in the first
three months of the season.

In 1995, Coe-Jones also became pregnant. The mom-to-be continued on the women's tour right up to the U.S. Open in July. Struggling with her burgeoning body and the hot summer weather, she still managed to tie for seventh spot.

"I don't know how I'm going to react to being a mom," she said when asked about her return date to the circuit. "It wouldn't shock me to hang up the clubs [for good], but it wouldn't shock me to play a minimum of 10 tournaments [in 1996]."

Coe-Jones ended up playing a lot more than she thought the next year. With her new son Jimmy on the road with her, Coe-Jones played 21 tournaments. Not surprisingly, her golf game suffered—after five straight seasons in the top 25 on the money list, she finished 54th, earning just over $120,000.

For the most part, she competed on the circuit without much help. Travelling with Jimmy by herself, Coe-Jones relied heavily on the LPGA's daycare facility at each tournament stop, allowing her time to practice and play in the event. Sleep deprivation and minimal time to work on her game took their toll.

With the responsibility of a new son, golf also became less of a priority. Even though she wasn't contemplating retirement, Coe-Jones planned to cut back on her schedule to spend more time at home.

For the next six seasons Coe-Jones averaged just over 20 tournaments per year, and while making enough to keep her playing card, she failed to have a top-three finish. During that period she played her best golf in Canada, at the du Maurier Classic. In 1998 Coe-Jones finished fourth, and the next year she shared the halfway lead at the event before faltering to end up in fifth place.

At that point, her son Jimmy was almost four, and Coe-Jones said she didn't want to be away from home when he started school. "I don't see myself playing a lot longer," she admitted during the 1998 du Maurier.

By 2002 she was playing fewer than 20 events per year and had only two top-10 results in her last seven seasons. She retired from competition in 2008 with career earnings topping $3.3 million.

Lisa Walters

When Lisa Walters won her first pro title in Hawaii just a week before Coe-Jones followed with her maiden victory, it fulfilled a dream that had started in Prince Rupert, BC, years earlier.

Born Lisa Young, the BC native grew up on a golf course. Her parents loved the sport, and they channeled the competitive juices of their daughter with hours of time on the driving range and practice green. When she won the BC junior title in 1977, Young was an intimidating presence. Bigger and stronger than most of the other girls, she hit the ball a long way and demolished the field.

She then added three BC amateur championships and earned a scholarship at Florida State University where she was an all-American in 1981. Two years later she nailed down a spot on the LPGA circuit with a 16th place finish at the final qualifying tournament.

She made a splash in her rookie season when she tied for fourth at the Rochester International and finished fifth at the LPGA Championship. She would end the year earning $53,411, which was good enough for 48th on the money list. Even though she was playing against the best players in the world, Young's strength still stood out. In her first season she was already recognized as one of the circuit's longest hitters.

She had another solid season in 1987 with a third-place finish at the McDonald's Championship, a total $72,074 in earnings that put her at 34th on the money list. Then came four years of frustration. Young slumped big time. She failed to crack $40,000 in earnings from 1988 to 1991. That's a total of 106 tournaments without a top-five finish.

In 1988, she won only $22,625. The year's bright spot came on the eve of the Kemper Open on Kauai when she married her long-time golf mentor Mike Walters. Dawn Coe was a witness at the civil ceremony.

"I guess 50 or 60 of the [LPGA} girls were there, too," said the new bride, now Lisa Walters after dropping her maiden name. "The ceremony wasn't actually on the beach; it was near it, on a lawn outside the hotel. After, we bought everyone a few drinks in the hotel. It's the way we wanted it. Quick and simple, with no expensive frills."

Mike Walters had been a former PGA touring pro, who had become a stockbroker after his playing days ended. The newlyweds made Tampa, Florida, their home. Walters hoped that marriage bliss would help her turn things around on the golf course, but her poor play continued.

"That four-year slump was just pitiful," she said about a stretch that had her finish each campaign no higher than 94th on the money list. "I was depressed, I was unhappy. I hated my life."

Then out of nowhere in 1992 came that final round 65 at the Itoki Hawaiian Ladies Open and her first LPGA triumph. She would call it a "fluke." Despite the five-year exemption from having to qualify on the Tour and the jump in her standing on the money list, Walters knew her swing needed revamping.

In the off-season, she spent some time with swing coach Fred Griffin. Under the watchful eye of her new coach, Walters developed a steady, repetitive swing she could rely on. She returned to the tour by defending her Hawaiian title and didn't miss a single cut through the entire season. She jumped up to 37th on the money list with $149,260.

Despite the breakthrough year, trouble was looming ahead. Walters had already had to persevere through four operations to repair ligament damage on her left knee. Then her right knee suffered the same problem. Then came two wrist operations. Her most serious setback—surgery to repair a ruptured disc in her lower back—limited Walters to only five tournaments in 1996.

"My husband gave me the okay to go ahead and quit after he got tired of all my complaining a couple of years ago," said Walters in 1998. "But then I decided, nah, I'll keep on playing."

In 1997, she played in 23 events and made only $26,976. Slowly her swing came back, and the next year, the 38-year-old had a remarkable comeback campaign. In June, she won the Oldsmobile Classic by six strokes to take her third LPGA title. Her 72-hole total of 23-under 265 tied the all-time women's scoring record.

"The last few years have been discouraging," she told the *Vancouver Sun* after the victory worth $97,500. "I always thought I was a better athlete than I was proving on the golf course. And that's very discouraging, to be banging your head against a wall year after year."

Walters had six top-10 results in 1998. She made the cut in 20 of 26 events and earned $308,933 to place her 25th on the money list.

"It would have been a great year any year to do what I did this year, but I know the quality of competition is really strong right now," she said referring to the new depth of talent in the LPGA pool, including Annika Sorenstam, Karrie Webb, Se Ri Pak, Liselotte Neumann and Dottie Pepper. "To me that makes it even more meaningful."

As the 1998 season wrapped up, Walters' wrist was once again aching. She predicted minor surgery would be waiting for her, but unfortunately, the "minor" surgery turned into two separate procedures on her left wrist and thumb. She sat out all of 1999 in an effort to completely rest and heal her hand.

Walters played in three tournaments to start the 2000 season and found the treatment she required to gear up for an event took longer than the time she had to practice. "My other hand started bothering me, my knees were bothering me and as soon as I came back on tour, my back, which had been pretty good since having surgery in 1996, started hurting again. I couldn't even get my ball out of the hole without it hurting."

Walters decided to listen to her body and retired after missing the cut at the Nabisco Championship in Rancho Mirage, California. She was disappointed to end her career prematurely, but took some solace in going out on top.

"I'm glad I finished on a good year," reflected Walters on a 17-year LPGA run that earned her just over $1 million. "It made my career a whole lot better having finished like that, for sure. But on the other hand, it would have been nice to go out there and expect to play like that for several more years."

Gail Graham

Three years after Coe-Jones graduated from Lamar University in 1983, Gail Graham left the same Texas college to begin a pro golfing career that would include two LPGA victories. Graham was born in Vanderhoof, BC, but grew up in Winnipeg where she began playing golf at age 13.

In 1983, she won the Manitoba Amateur Championship (a title she won again in 1985) and was the low amateur at the 1987 du Maurier Classic. After turning pro in 1988, she competed on the Futures Tour and a year later placed fifth at the LPGA final qualifying tournament to earn her playing card.

After struggling for three years with only one top-10 result, Graham earned over $100,000 for the first time in 1993, including a third-place finish at the Sun-Times Challenge. In the off season, Graham made a major change to her swing, and it paid off in 1994, when she had five top-10 results and made $124,000 to finish 40th on the money list.

In 1995, the five-foot-three, brown-haired Canadian won the Fieldcrest Cannon Classic by recording four rounds in the 60s. Graham led going into the final round, but was passed by Tammie Green who birdied two of the first four holes. It wasn't until the 15th hole that Graham regained the lead.

On the par-5 18th, Graham reached the green in two shots, while Green was on in three. For the first time all day, the Canadian began to get nervous and hit her first putt 11 feet past the hole. When Green missed her birdie putt, Graham had two putts to nail down the victory.

Coe-Jones was the first person to call and congratulate Graham on her first LPGA triumph. "She said something to the effect that 'now wasn't that easy,' and when I thought about it later, it actually was."

The victory was worth $75,000 and propelled Graham to another top-50 finish on the money list with $142,000. Her effervescent personality and keen mind—she was an NCAA Academic All-American at Lamar—made her an ideal candidate to become a member of the LPGA Executive Committee. As a member of the tour's six-player board of directors, she had input on such decisions as finding a new LPGA commissioner.

"It's kind of exciting, being in on many of the decisions in the overall tour operations," said Graham on her involvement with the committee. "We have quite a bit of input into things, with player interaction, sponsors and tour staff."

After a disappointing 1998, when she slipped to 52nd on the money list with just over $122,000, Graham rebounded the next season with her best showing on the circuit. She earned $223,040, including her second win at the Alpine Australian Ladies Masters. The victory was worth

$97,500 and propelled her to a career-best 32nd place finish in LPGA earnings for 1999.

In 2001, she failed to have a top-10 placing for the first time in nine seasons and made less than $20,000. A year earlier Graham had been elected president of the LPGA, a time-consuming position that started her thinking about the transition from player to another golf-related career.

Graham retired from full-time play at the end of the 2003 season with just under $1.3 million in career earnings. She started work as a part-time golf commentator and a tour consultant. Graham is currently president of the LPGA Tournament Owners Association, a non-profit organization made up of LPGA sanctioned tournament owners and operators who are working together to grow their tour.

Jennifer Wyatt

The fourth member of the BC contingent was another graduate of Lamar University. Jennifer Wyatt played five years for the collegiate team and won two individual titles during her time in Texas.

Wyatt grew up in Richmond, BC, and first gained attention in local golfing circles when she won the 1983 Women's Western Junior Golf Championship. The next year, she won the BC Junior title and was ranked as Canada's second best junior golfer.

Following in the footsteps of Coe-Jones and Graham, Wyatt signed up sight-unseen to play at Lamar. "At the beginning of the year it was intimidating," said Wyatt after her first season in Beaumont, Texas. "But there was a steady improvement. I started in the 80s, then got into a routine and started playing better."

In 1985, Wyatt followed up an improved second season at Lamar with a second-place finish at the Canadian Women's Amateur Championship. For the next three years she was the number-one ranked amateur player in the country, and in 1987 won the New Zealand Amateur Championship and a gold medal at the Commonwealth Games as part of the four-member Canadian team.

Even before graduating with a degree in graphic design in 1988, Wyatt had decided to aim for the LPGA Tour. Her first attempt at qualifying in 1989 was a wild up-and-down ride.

"The first qualifying in Wichita I missed by four strokes," said the 23-year-old. "Then I went to Venice [Florida]. I made it by two shots. I birdied the last two holes. I never shook like that before in my life."

Next Wyatt moved on to the final qualifying test in Sweetwater, Texas. After a nightmarish 86 during the third round, Wyatt rebounded to shoot a final round 73, which was good enough for non-exempt status, allowing her to play in 21 events in her first LPGA season.

As a rookie, she managed a pair of top-10 finishes, including fourth place at the Atlantic City Classic. Wyatt made $31,794 in total earnings, good enough for 82nd place on the money list. It was an encouraging start to her pro career, but in 1990, Wyatt took a step backwards, the unfortunate victim of the sophomore jinx.

"I can't say my 1989 success was a fluke," reflected Wyatt on what happened after her rookie season, "but it was rather scatterbrained. There are a lot of distractions on tour; it's not all glamorous. There is a lot of travel, and playing every week can be kind of a drag. I wanted instant progress, I guess, and I was forgetting my swing. When you lose your swing, you lose your confidence."

When the final numbers were in for the season, Wyatt had slipped to 103rd on the money list, making $31,631. "I missed a helluva of a lot of cuts," she said about a season that had only one top-10 result. "I wanted to quit. I was so mad."

Wyatt headed to Australia after the LPGA season ended to play a couple of tournaments and get some help with her swing. She also made a lifestyle change, buying her own apartment in Sarasota, Florida, to avoid the long trip to Vancouver between LPGA events.

The move seemed to pay immediate dividends early in the next season as she won almost $50,000 and had a third place finish in the PING Cellular One Championship. In 1992, she had her best season as a pro, earning $104,078 in prize money and her only PGA title at the Crestar Farm Fresh Classic. For the next five seasons, Wyatt struggled, barely topping $40,000 in her best seasons. After playing four tournaments in 1998, she decided to call it quits.

"Basically I wasn't making any money," explained Wyatt about her decision, "and I've never been in debt, and I didn't want to start now. And it didn't make any sense for me to stay in Florida."

Wyatt moved back to BC and began teaching golf. Not surprisingly she has become a well-respected coach and instructor.

Chapter Seven

Richard Zokol

"Disco Dick"

Born Kitimat, BC, 1958–

His goals were modest when Richard Zokol started taking golf seriously as a teenager on the west side of Vancouver. His father, Joe Zokol, was a member of the Marine Drive Golf Club, the home of many of the province's best players. Richard, the youngest of the Zokol's four children, wanted to raise his game to the standard set by Marine Drive's finest golfers.

"I wanted so badly to be a part of the fraternity of good players at Marine," said Zokol in Arv Olson's, *Backspin, a History of Golf in BC.* "I realized I'd have to work hard to belong. I was proud of the club's tradition. I wanted my name with all those others on that plaque of champions in the clubhouse."

Ironically, Zokol, never became club champion. Instead, he ended up as PGA regular, with two titles to his credit in a career that spanned 15 seasons. In a sport where it's sometimes a difficult task to find a colourful personality, Zokol stood out. He forged his golfing career in his own unique manner, and he was always quite willing to share his ideas with anyone who asked.

Zokol was born in Kitimat, a small town in western BC not far from Prince Rupert. As a youngster, Richard took up sports with an intense energy that made him a star on the soccer pitch and the baseball diamond.

When his father started a dentistry practice in Vancouver, Richard began caddying at Marine Drive. The 13-year-old fell in with the wrong crowd, and when his father discovered that his son was smoking marijuana with his new friends, Joe grounded him for a year; the only place he was allowed to go was the golf course.

For the next 12 months, Zokol caddied, cleaned clubs, picked up balls on the driving range, scrubbed toilets and worked as a busboy in the dining room. He also found time to play, and just as important, watched how the club's best players approached the game. Zokol observed how Doug

Roxburgh, one of the country's all-time great amateur players, dedicated himself to the sport.

"Learning the game in that intensely competitive environment was so stimulating. Watching Roxburgh, trying to emulate him, probably was the biggest impact on my game. Everyone admired Doug for his ethics and behaviour. There was total affinity to him as a pure ball-striker."

When he was 14, Zokol was scheduled to be the starting pitcher for the Kerrisdale All-Stars in their league opener at Little Mountain Park. It was then that the youngster made a life-changing decision.

"Jack Westover had asked me to caddie for him in the Sun Match Play tournament. And that was the absolute instant moment that I committed to golf. I said I would rather caddie for a golf pro in a tournament than play this other sport. A lot of people thought I was crazy. I remember my baseball coach saying, 'You're what?'"

By the time he was 15, Zokol had quit all other sports, except high school soccer, to concentrate on golf. At the 1976 BC junior tourney, he finished tied for second and followed that up the next year with wins at the City Amateur and Greenacres Amateur events where he beat Roxburgh and several of the province's best amateurs.

At the BC amateur later that summer, Zokol led through the first three rounds, before double bogeying on the back nine to finish third. During the first two rounds, he was teamed with Jim Nelford, another local golfer who had won back-to-back Canadian Amateurs and was about to turn professional. Nelford recommended Zokol to Karl Tucker, the golf coach at Brigham Young University.

Zokol borrowed his father's car and drove 24 hours to Utah to show Tucker that he had some potential. Tucker was sufficiently impressed, helping Zokol earn a partial scholarship at BYU. Under Tucker's tutelage, he began to smooth out what had been a choppy swing. By his senior year, Zokol had improved enough to earn the team captaincy, and in 1981, led Brigham Young to its first NCAA Championship.

Later that summer, Zokol won the biggest title of his amateur career when he defeated Blaine McAllister in a sudden-death playoff to win the Canadian Amateur tournament at the Calgary Golf and Country Club. He turned pro later that fall when he earned a spot on the PGA Tour by finishing tied for the last available spot at qualifying school.

In his first 11 years as a professional, Zokol had to repeat the grind of qualifying five times. It was a slow and often frustrating process; one that is not unusual in the playing ranks of the PGA where it takes years to figure out how to become a consistently good golfer.

As a rookie in 1983, Zokol earned mention in newspapers and magazines across North America when he shared the lead at the Greater Milwaukee Open with only four holes to play. Zokol had shot rounds of 65, 69 and 70, but made the headlines for listening to his portable music player between shots.

When reporters asked him the purpose of the portable stereo, Zokol explained he was trying to block out negative thoughts and emotions. When they asked him what he listened to, the Tour rookie said he favoured FM music and news. With the double-bogey on the final round, Zokol shot a 75, which was good enough for fifth place.

"All of the sudden, I felt so uncomfortable," said Zokol when describing how he faltered near the end of the final round. "My anxiety made it hard for me to hit good shots. I was a product of the situation. It was controlling me rather than the other way around. I didn't know what to do with my excitement."

It was his highest finish in his first year on the Tour, and Zokol had definitely made his mark with the media, who called him "Disco Dick." The headset lasted only a couple of seasons as Zokol searched for a better way to control his anxiety. Searching out new methods to relax on the course, Zokol visited Richard Lonetto, a University of Guelph psychology professor who convinced him there were more subtle methods.

When Lonetto watched Zokol play at a tournament in New Hampshire, he witnessed a golfer who wasn't sure what shot to play as he stood over the ball. Indecisiveness equals anxiety, so Lonetto convinced Zokol to develop a pre-shot routine that would slow down his heart rate. Called a deep-breathing bio-rhythm procedure, Lonetto had Zokol lift his club shoulder high, while addressing each shot. He pointed the club to the sky while taking a deep breath and slowly exhaled. Before going into the back swing, Zokol would take his right hand off the club and extend his arm from his side.

After building Zokol's routine in a step-by-step manner, Lonetto also wanted Zokol to not be distracted by what was going on around him. The goal was to quiet his mind so he could focus on each shot.

Zokol told Canadian golf writer Lorne Rubenstein that he is at his best when he plays "cold-blooded golf." "It is about avoiding the emotional ups and downs; it's about getting the job done," he explained. "If I hit a 1-iron two feet from the hole I don't react. The ball doesn't care that I've hit it that close. I've got the next shot to play. That's all that matters."

He struggled to earn a living in his first few seasons. Despite the good result in Milwaukee, Zokol made just $15,110 in his 1982 rookie season. The next year he improved to $38,107. In 1984, he won $15,000 in his first Tour event, but then things deteriorated as he started missing cuts.

In desperation, Zokol gave up friendships because he believed he was relying on them too much for support. He fired caddies when he thought he was too wrapped up with their problems. He even miscalculated yardage on one hole, a mortal sin for a PGA professional. These were all signs that Zokol seemed to be falling apart.

But as the season progressed, he slowly began climbing the earnings ladder. In 1985, he made $71,000, but the next season was a disaster as he barely topped $35,000. He lost his touring card again and was the 50th and last man to make it back to the Tour in qualifying school.

In 1987, he topped a $100,000 in official money for the first time. In July, he made a run for a Canadian Open title. Zokol was the co-leader with Curtis Strange and Mike McCullough at nine under par heading into the final round. Severe thunderstorms forced the Canadian to play 36 holes on Saturday, and he responded with rounds of 68 and 69 to move up the leaderboard.

Zokol felt the expectations of an entire country during the final round, as he stumbled to a 75 to finish in seventh place. He bogeyed the first, seventh and ninth holes and played par the rest of the day.

"I'm not a super-experienced golfer; I've only been there [among the leaders] a few times, and I couldn't get calmed down," summed up Zokol afterwards. "I just didn't handle the situation as well as I wanted. Basically, we're not playing golf out there, we're playing mind games, and it's the one who can control himself the best who wins."

In 1988, he jumped to $142,000 in earnings despite the addition of twin boys, Conor and Garrett. Rather than leave the three-month-old toddlers at home with wife Joan, the Zokol's decided to take the family on the road.

"Some people may think I'm crazy, that I won't be able to play well with Joan and the boys along," Zokol said in an interview just before the start of the 1988 season. "Things will work out, because we want them to work out. We're a family. We don't want to be away from each other."

For each tournament stop, the Zokol's rented a condominium or a hotel suite with adjoining rooms so Richard could get some proper sleep. For events more than 1200 kilometres apart, the family made the trip by airplane, while Zokol's caddie drove the van with the playpens, toys, diapers and clothes.

"The first thing I used to consider deciding on a tournament appearance was the golf course," said Zokol. "After this year, the courses could be second in importance to the daycare provisions."

Family life suited Zokol just fine. In 1990, he increased his earnings to $191,000. He had several top-10 finishes, including two second-place finishes at tourneys in Tennessee and Hawaii.

In 1992, Zokol broke through to win two events. His first victory came at the Deposit Guaranty Golf Classic in Hattiesburg, Mississippi, during the same week as the Masters. Even though the win was classified as nonofficial because the Tour's top golfers were playing at Augusta, the victory earned Zokol $54,000 in prize money and was a validation of all the work he had done to curb his emotions on the golf course.

"I'd said to my caddie at the beginning of the week that we should be sharp," said Zokol after the win. "I'd been playing well, but I hadn't put the ball-striking and putting together in the same week. But I felt good about all parts of my game coming in. My goal was to be alert, to give myself every opportunity to win."

Before the year ended, Zokol added a second victory, the Greater Milwaukee Open, in a full PGA field. This time his trademark headphones were long gone as he fired a five-under 67 on the same course where he earned the nickname "Disco Dick" a decade earlier. Zokol finished at 19 under par, two strokes ahead of the field.

In 1982, Zokol was the leader heading into the final round; 10 years later he started Sunday's round a stroke behind defending champion Mark Brooks. Five straight birdies put Zokol ahead to stay as Brooks fell apart on the 18th with a triple bogey.

"I had a lot of lucky breaks coming in and basically had it handed to me on a silver platter," said Zokol about the final round. "And I'll take it, thank you very much."

"I'm the kind of person who in the past probably got the worst out of my game. It's a lack of focus that did that."

Zokol earned $180,000 for the victory, and just as importantly, he tucked away a two-year Tour exemption and added invitations to the

1993 Masters, Tournament of Champions, World Series and the PGA Championship. The win lifted his yearly earnings to over $300,000 for the first time in his career.

"This tournament is very special to me," said Zokol. "This is where Disco Dick debuted; the first time I got into contention on the PGA Tour."

For almost half his schedule, Zokol's wife, Joan, and their now three young children (daughter Hayley was the third addition) travelled together to each Tour stop. Living on the west coast of Canada made the trips even more daunting.

"When I told a couple of players we had left home at 6:00 AM and got to our hotel in the east at 9:00 PM, they didn't believe me," said Zokol about bringing the family along on an eastern swing. They thought I'd come from Alaska or the Yukon, or something."

Even while reaching his prime playing years, Zokol knew that pro golf could be a fleeting career. His plan was to play for a few more years, hopefully banking between $300,000 and $400,000 a year while looking for other career options.

"I don't want to sacrifice my family life to pay the bills," he explained. "There's so many players in their 40s out there who have to play and have trouble making cuts. It's an awful lifestyle, and they've got nothing to fall back on. That won't be Dick Zokol. I want to have a choice."

Zokol lost his exempt status on the Tour after the 1994 season. Zokol the golfer gradually gave away to Zokol the entrepreneur. He starred on his own golf show and had a regular column in the *Vancouver Sun*. He became an executive involved in course design for a large property firm called Intrawest Corporation of Vancouver. He was even featured in ads for Esquire watches.

"I am looking after the needs of my family," he said about his decision to focus less on golf. "A lot of people think that because I am Richard Zokol I must be well off, but I am not."

"The two good years [1992–93] that I've had don't mean anything. I have to put my nose to the grindstone."

He continued to play professional golf at events like the Canadian Open and the Greater Vancouver Open where he received invitational exemptions, but his heart wasn't into leaving home for long stretches of time. At the 1997 Greater Vancouver Open, he stayed in contention well into the final round. Riding the goodwill of a hometown gallery, Zokol was within two strokes of the lead right up to the 14th hole before he faded over the last few holes to finish 12th. Despite a limited playing schedule, Zokol was still encouraged by the fact he had been able to successfully compete against a PGA field.

With his kids growing up, Zokol decided he had enough good golf left in him to give the PGA Tour one last go. The first step was becoming a regular on the 2001 Buy.com Tour, then he had to finish in the top 15 on the money list to earn a ticket to the big show.

Zokol started the marathon season well, winning the Canadian PGA Championship in Toronto and following that up with a number of solid tournaments, missing only one of his first 18 cuts. He was well positioned to finish in the top 15, but the long season caught up with him. He started to sputter and was forced to play non-stop golf for over two months to protect his position.

At the season-ending Buy.com Tour Championship, he tied for 39th, which was enough for him to finish the year 13th on the money list with earnings of $167,192. It was the Canadian golf comeback story of the year.

"I've played a lot of good golf this year," he said. "I've had a bit of a flame-out the last couple of weeks. Mentally, I'm exhausted. But I'm not going to let that spoil what has been a great year for me."

"The commitment to come back and play full-time and go this route is massive. I can feel very good about that. I can say that I have been very humbled by not being on the PGA Tour for seven years, and I've learned a lot from it. I took being out there for granted."

Zokol was especially proud that his children were able to watch their father at work. His sons were only five and his daughter just two when he had his best year in 1992.

"I'm thoroughly enjoying myself," he said about his resurgence. "Regardless of what happens, I feel very comfortable with who I am, where I'm at and how I'm playing. My maturity level is good, I guess. Golf is not such a serious thing now."

Zokol ended up playing 20 PGA events in the 2002 season. But the magic that propelled him back to the top suddenly deserted him as Zokol won only $53,437 and failed to crack the top 10 in any of the tournaments he played in. With the loss of his PGA playing card, Zokol was invited to only 10 events in 2003, and by 2005, he retired from competition to concentrate on his many business interests.

Chapter Eight

Dave Barr

Mr. Consistency

Born Kelowna, BC, 1952–

Dave Barr made a living playing golf. He wasn't one to talk about the pastoral scenery of a special course, the intricacies of the swing or his place in the long history of the sport. Instead, Dave Barr slogged out a livelihood on the PGA circuit. In 17 straight seasons, he made enough on the Tour to avoid the dreaded qualifying school. He was the quintessential grinder; never was there an ounce of flashiness or flamboyance about his game.

To watch Barr at work was to see someone who didn't seem to be having much fun. A round of golf was something of a test of survival, his stoic countenance only broken by irritation of a shot gone wrong or a member of the gallery making a sound at an inopportune moment.

Take for example the 1986 BC Open at the Point Grey Golf Club in Vancouver, the gallery hushed as Barr, looking like someone who woke up on the wrong side of the bed, prepared to hit his next shot. Suddenly, he stepped away from the ball and stared directly into the crowd.

"Sir," the six-foot-one, 195-pound golfer growled, "would you please stop jingling that change in your pocket."

Like or dislike his all-business approach, Dave Barr made more money than any other Canadian golfer before him. He was the first Canuck to surpass $2 million in Tour winnings while taking two PGA titles. In 1985, he was the runner-up in the U.S. Open, bogeying the two final holes after leading by two strokes with only six holes to play.

Dave Barr grew up in the Okanagan area of British Columbia. His parents encouraged their two sons to play sports, and Dave excelled at baseball and hockey (he played for a Junior B team in Kelowna).

Neither his mother nor father played golf. Only after he became a ball-hunter (finding lost golf balls and selling them back to the golf course for 50 to 75 cents) did he develop an interest in the game.

When he was 12-years-old, he began caddying at the Kelowna Golf and Country Club. He was a right-hander, but the only clubs available to him were lefties, so Barr learned the game by using a cross-handed grip. The next year, he received his aunt's clubs and was able to swing right-handed. He spent hours hitting golf balls in a local school-yard and then playing on municipal golf courses.

His parents dropped him off at the local course at 6:00 AM, and 54 holes later at 9:00 PM, would pick him up. By the time he was 15, Barr had made himself into a three-handicap player. He was self-taught in the true sense of the word; throughout his entire career, he never had a swing coach. This explains why Barr learned the game with an unorthodox baseball grip (the so-called 10-finger grip), while almost all of his peers were taught the overlapping or interlocking grips.

His one glaring weakness was his hook, but by adjusting his grip and swing, Barr improved enough to join three other Canadians on the golf team at Oral Roberts University in Tulsa, Okla-homa. He was there on a one-year conditional scholarship, but that was soon lengthened to four full years when he became the number two player on the university team. In 1973, he fin-ished fifth behind the winner, Ben Crenshaw, in the NCAA Championship tournament and was runner-up at the Canadian Amateur. He was rewarded for his runner-up finish with an invitation to play at the World Amateur team championships in Argentina.

He turned pro in 1973 but struggled for two years on the Canadian circuit. His first breakthrough came in 1975 when he won the BC Open, worth $4000. Barr was able to make ends meet when his brother formed Red Ink Inc., a group of sponsors that helped with his expenses. The BC Open prize money was the first indication that Dave might not be such a bad investment after all.

It was still a tough go. During the winter months Barr put the golf clubs away to work in the SunRype juice plant in Kelowna; often relegated to the graveyard cleanup shift. In 1976, he married his childhood sweetheart, LuAnn Busch, who worked to keep them financially afloat while Barr concentrated on improving his golf game.

He tried qualifying for the PGA Tour in 1976, but didn't get past the first round. The next year he won some money on the Arizona winter mini-tour and then played in smaller events across Canada and into the United States. It paid off as Barr won $19,000 by capturing the BC, Alberta, Québec and Washington State Open tournaments. To finish off a great season, Barr qualified for the PGA Tour by finishing 25th at the final Q-school event (the top 25 players and ties made it).

With another group of sponsors backing him, Barr struggled during his first year on the Tour, but made enough cuts to retain his card. He scraped by over the next three years, fighting his putting, his temper and his hook to make enough money to avoid Q-school. It was a tough time. In his first five years on the Tour, he made less than $100,000 in official earnings.

In 1981, at the Quad Cities Open, Barr finally had his breakthrough, winning the tournament and earning a four-year PGA exemption. It wasn't easy though. He shot a final round 66 to come back from a five-shot deficit, joining four other pros in a playoff that lasted eight extra holes at the Oakwood Country Club in Coal Harbor, Illinois. He managed a par on the eighth extra hole to win the second longest playoff in PGA history. At the time it seemed the big Canadian had his breakthrough win, but the title proved to be more of a burden.

"I put a lot of pressure on myself after winning that tournament," Barr said a year later. "Everybody was expecting me to do so much more. I added that pressure on to myself, thinking those thoughts."

Perhaps he could have relaxed a little, knowing that he had a guaranteed spot on the Tour for the next four years, but Barr struggled during the 1982 season, winning only $12,474. Things got worse when he hurt his left shoulder while carrying luggage, and he began waking up with headaches and neck pain. The rest of the season, he played only seven of 13 tournaments. In 1983, the slump continued as he finished 166th on the money list.

"I was making the cuts, but I really wasn't playing very well, making only $700 or $800 a week." said a frustrated Barr in describing his slump. "I kept hitting it good but couldn't putt, and putting is the name of the game on tour."

The next year, things began to improve as he jumped over a 100 spots to place 62nd in earnings. With his exemption about to expire after 1985, Barr notched his game up another level.

At the 1985 U.S. Open at the famed Oakland Hills course in Detroit, Barr put together three solid rounds of 70, 68 and 70. His 208 total put him in third place, three shots behind Andy North and five behind T.C. Chen of Taiwan.

Chen faltered early in the final round by taking a quadruple-bogey eight at the fifth hole, while Barr birdied the hole. For a short time on the back nine, Barr held a two-stroke lead, but his driver began to go awry. When Barr and North arrived at the 17th tee they were tied for the lead. There was a stiff crosswind to contend with; Barr had the honours and decided with 204 yards to the hole that a three-iron was the right club.

"I was unlucky having the honour on that particular hole with the wind gusting," he later recalled. "I would have taken a four-iron had I seen [playing partner Rick] Fehr's shot first." Instead Barr's shot zipped through the green and nestled in some deep rough behind the green, 40 feet from the cup

Barr was forced into making a difficult flop shot; the ball ended up on the green, but still 40 feet from the hole, and he ended up with a two-putt for a bogey. On the 18th, a 450-yard, par-four monster, Barr decided to play for a par and hope North faltered to force a playoff.

Still hitting into the wind, Barr tried to hit beside a bunker about 260 yards out, but his ball found the sand. His luck continued to sour on his second shot, "I gambled with a four-iron to clear the lip of the bunker. I just clipped it, taking everything off the shot and came up 100 yards short of the green."

Barr recovered on this third shot, hitting a fantastic pitch to within eight feet of the cup. North had also struggled on the hole, and if Barr was able to sink the putt, he would force a playoff. His McGregor blade putter sent the ball right on target, but the little white sphere didn't cooperate; it circled the hole and stayed out to give North his second U.S. Open title.

Barry McDermott's June 24th article in *Sports Illustrated* described Barr's decline: "For a brief spell on the back nine Sunday Barr held a two-stroke lead, but he must have realized this wasn't the Quad Cities Open, and from then on his whippy backswing looked like a slicing machine gone mad. He staggered in, bogeying the final two holes and failing to hit five of the last six greens. 'The monster bit back today,' said Barr, referring to Oakland Hills' nickname."

Afterwards Barr insisted his second place finish would not be a setback. "That week was reassuring for me. It told me I could still be competitive in that company."

He was right. Over the next several seasons, Barr remained a competitive golfer on the circuit, amassing enough good results to finish safely in the middle of the earnings pack. The closest he came to a PGA title in that time was in 1986 when he lost a playoff to Corey Pavin at the Milwaukee Open.

The six-year winless drought ended in 1987. His putter was like a magic wand, as Barr shot a final round 65 to run away with the Atlanta Classic, finishing with a 23-under 265 total, for his second PGA victory.

"It's such a super feeling, it's hard to describe," said Barr after the final round. "You wonder if you're ever going to win again. I really didn't feel the pressure. I had the inner calm where I had everything under control."

"The Quad Cities was a long time ago," he mused afterwards. "But some close finishes, like my tie for second in the '85 U.S. Open, kept me going and kept my hopes alive."

In 1988, he lost another playoff at the Greater Hartford Open to Mark Brooks. Barr had shot a tournament best 63 in the final round to earn his way into the playoff. On the second extra hole he made a miraculous chip shot that made the sports highlight packages on television stations across North America. Reversing his sand wedge while having to switch to a left-handed stance, Barr hit a third-shot chip from an almost impossible spot (on railroad ties used to support the slope at the edge of a water hazard) and pulled the shot off as the ball rolled close to the pin.

Unfortunately for Barr, Brooks had hit his approach shot on the par-4, 399-yard 17th hole to within 10 feet of the cup and nailed the birdie putt for the win. "You hate to lose a playoff, but it was a birdie, so Mark earned it," said Barr to reporters after earning $61,600 for the second place showing. "I was never given the chance to putt."

Things really became exciting later that summer, when Barr was in contention at the Canadian Open. Bad weather had plagued the event, but on Sunday night, Barr was the clubhouse leader, finishing at 11-under.

With several players still on the course, the tournament was postponed until the next morning. Ken Green was 12-under, but had only finished 12 holes. The next day the weather was still miserable, but Green and the others were able to complete their rounds. Green ended up going one-under on the remaining holes to win at 13-under.

Barr reached the pinnacle of his golfing career during a three-year stretch that ended in 1988. Nagging back problems and erratic putting slowed him down in subsequent years. In 1994, however, Barr was back in the headlines as he captained the Canadian team to the Alfred Dunhill Cup championship.

It was an unlikely victory—Barr had slipped in the world rankings to 170th. His teammates, Rick Gibson (ranked 215th) and Ray Stewart (452nd) were even farther down the ladder. An 80–1 long shot to take the title, the Canadians prevailed over 15 other countries in the tournament. The Canuck threesome outlasted such PGA stars as Ernie Els, Bernhard Langer, Nick Price, David Frost, Tom Kite, Jesper Parnevik and Curtis Strange.

The tournament was held on the Old Course at St. Andrews, Scotland. Barr won a couple of huge matches in the preliminary rounds, defeating Price and Langer to send Canada into the semi-finals for the first time in the tournament's 10-year history. "Dave inspired us," said Stewart, who along with Gibson, won their semi-final match to take the heat off of Barr who lost to Els.

In the finals, the upstart Canadians were pitted against the powerhouse American team, consisting of Curtis Strange, Tom Kite and Fred Couples. It would not be easy as the U.S. threesome had 47 PGA Tour wins and four major championships among them.

Barr opened with a huge win over Kite, putting pressure on the American favourites. Strange defeated Gibson by seven strokes. Stewart jumped out to a great start against Couples (who was then the 6th ranked player in the world) and led by two-shots after 15 holes.

"I was on the 16th green, when they posted Dave's victory," said Stewart, who had two second-place finishes on the PGA Tour during his career. "I said to myself: 'Now it's up to me.'"

And the BC golfer came through with a one-stroke victory over Couples. The three Canadians each won $216,000 for the victory, and perhaps for the first time in his pro career, Barr was overcome with emotion on the golf course.

"It was a victory of major proportions and one I will remember the rest of my life," Barr said later. "For me it was a very emotional day. I'm so proud to have a victory representing my country. That's why I had a tear in my eye."

Barr's great victory in Scotland, however, didn't count as a PGA Tour event, and for the first time in 18 years, he was forced back to qualifying school to earn his card. Barr didn't finish near the top in the five-round endurance test and played only 16 PGA tournaments the next year thanks to sponsor exemptions and getting into draws as an alternate.

Barr never regained his status as a PGA regular, but between some exemptions to Tour events and his appearances at Canadian Tour events, he kept his game sharp until 2003, when at the age of 50, he qualified to play on the Champions Tour. As a golf rookie again, Barr had a terrific season, winning $731,725 and finishing 27th on the money list. On the very competitive Senior circuit only the top 30 players get to keep their card.

In the first full-field event of the 2003 season, Barr made a splash by winning the Royal Caribbean Golf Classic in Florida. In the next two weeks he added 12th and seventh place finishes, leaving an impression that the Champions Tour would be an easy way to add to this retirement fund.

Over the remaining 25 events, Barr garnered only two top-10 placements and just managed to hold on to his card. "I don't want to make a long run of the Senior Tour," said Barr after his first season. "It's a tough road to get out here, and now that I'm out here, I'd just like to keep myself exempt for a couple of years and hopefully, maybe retire at an early age. You know, like Freedom 55."

In 2004, Barr finished his second season on the Champions Tour with $436,531 in earnings, which was only good enough for 46th place on the money list. By finishing in the top 50, he retained some status to play in about a dozen tournaments a year. Barr found the grind of the senior circuit even tougher than the PGA, and despite pocketing $1.16 million in two seasons, was almost relieved his schedule was cut back.

"It's disappointing, but it's not the end of the world," said Barr. "A lot of things are happening out here, and it's just not that much fun any more."

Barr has eased himself off the Champions Tour since he lost his full-time status in 2004.

As he faded from the golfing limelight, his legacy to some was of a brooding, ill-tempered introvert who alienated many fans. In evaluating Barr's accomplishments in the sport, however, many observers forget that the Kelowna resident was a self-taught golfer who developed his own unorthodox swing and style.

"I never relied on anybody," Barr said in a 1988 *Vancouver Sun* profile. "I just tried to stick with the fundamentals of the game. I think most of the time you can simply play through your problems. A lot of guys on the Tour worry too much about mechanics. If something goes wrong, they want a quick fix—instant success."

"When you think about it," the late Shaughnessy pro Jack McLaughlin said in evaluating Barr's place in golf, "it's really amazing what Dave has done with a swing most people thought couldn't stand up under that kind of pressure. He's been great for Canadian golf."

Besides being a role model for a younger generation of Canadian golfers, Barr supported national events throughout his career. Each season he would forego more lucrative PGA tournaments to play the Canadian circuit; he was a regular participant at the Manitoba Open, the Québec Open and the Canadian PGA Championship.

Friends and family members who know Barr best insist that the guy with the meaty hands and the constantly tanned face has always been generous and approachable. And while he admits to being a fierce competitor, Barr has said that he had to be that way to survive on the PGA circuit. For 17 straight seasons he kept his tour spot, while finishing no higher than 33rd on the money list—$291,244 in 1988.

"I'm a consistent (36-hole) cut-maker," Barr once said in describing his talents and place on the Tour. "I'm one of the grinders."

Chapter Nine

Jocelyne Bourassa
Rebel Golfer

Born Shawinigan, Québec, 1947–

When she burst on to the golfing scene in 1972, Jocelyne Bourassa had already established a reputation as a bit of an outlaw, who was more concerned about having fun than following the structured protocol of her chosen sport.

"I got into trouble," she recalled about her early days as one of Canada's best golfing prospects. "I was barred from the world team in 1968 because I preferred to go out with my boyfriend rather than go to a [Canadian Amateur] tournament awards banquet. The thing was, I didn't know I'd won anything."

"Once I was barred from a team because I showed up in my slacks at the course. Heaven for bid!" she added in mock horror.

►— —◄

Jocelyne Bourassa was born on May 30, 1947, in the town of Shawinigan, Québec. Her father never played golf, but he was able to recognize his children's interest in the game, sometimes setting up tomato cans in the backyard so Jocelyne and her older brother, Gilles, could practice their chipping. Gilles turned out to be a gifted golfer, winning the Québec junior title at age 18 (Jocelyne caddied).

"We are a close family," said Gilles about the dedication required by his father to help both his children through the junior ranks of golf. "Our father worked hard all his life [Léger Bourassa was a master electrician], and giving us money for golf was not easy. But he understood this life was what both of us wanted."

At the age of 13, Jocelyne joined the Ki-8-Eb Club in Trois-Rivières. She won her first tournament the same year. Her rise through the amateur ranks was amazingly swift; at the age of 16 she won her first of three consecutive Québec Junior titles and added the Québec Amateur championship (a title she also won in 1969 and 1971).

At 18, she won the Canadian Ladies Amateur Championship, and two years later, she won her first international title by taking the 1967 Scottish Girls Open Stroke Play Championship. Bourassa was beginning to be noticed in

Canadian golfing circles; not only for her ability, but also for the flair she exhibited on the course.

Fans loved her energy and emotion. Some of the more serious-minded officials frowned at her open displays of joy and frustration, but Bourassa had developed a following, especially in her home province of Québec.

In 1971, she dominated the amateur scene in Canada. With Gilles as her coach (he became a teaching pro at the age of 20), Jocelyne won the Ontario championship, repeated her Québec win by an amazing 14 strokes and then took her second Canadian Amateur title. She followed that up by winning the New Zealand Ladies' Best Ball Championship with partner Marilyn Palmer.

Bourassa had also graduated with a degree in physical education at the Université de Montréal and spent a year working toward her Master's in sociology of sport at the University of Wisconsin. At the age of 24, she had no more to accomplish in amateur golf; she was ready to become the second Canadian to join the LPGA Tour.

When she announced her intention to turn pro, things came together quickly. In those days, a player had to prove to the LPGA that she had at least $2400 in the bank (emergency funds in case things became financially difficult). A Montréal sportswriter wrote Jean-Louis Levesque, multi-millionaire owner of Windsor Raceway on behalf of Bourassa, to tell him about her situation.

Levesque called Bourassa and asked the young golfer if she was willing to make the sacrifices required to become a successful professional. Bourassa was prepared for the question: "I have thought about it a lot, Mr. Levesque," she replied. "If I get the chance, I'll give it everything I've got. I have even studied the LPGA rules, and I won't get any $50 fine for throwing a club, and I'll avoid the $50 fine for swearing by swearing only in French."

Levesque was charmed by her answer and told her to get things organized (it was December) so she was ready to start in January. He promised her $10,000 with no strings attached. "You keep any money you win," said Levesque, "but if you do well on the tour, I want you to help some other deserving girl sometime. And if time permits, you might help lower the grim handicap of my Jeanne [Mrs. Levesque]."

Bourassa rushed her application into the LPGA so she could play the Burdine Invitational in Doral, Florida, in the first week of January 1972. She had to make some big life changes over just a few short days. She had a serious boyfriend at the time; he was informed that marriage wasn't in the cards for at least a couple of years. She quit her job teaching at the Montreal YMCA. And she acquired an agent—the same business representative that handled sports legends Gordie Howe, Jean Beliveau, Rusty Staub and Nancy Greene.

With everything in place, Bourassa should have been excited about embarking on her LPGA adventure. Instead, the young golfer found it hard to leave home. "Something seemed to be holding me back at the door," remembered Bourassa in saying her final goodbyes to family and friends, "but I felt if I didn't take the big step through it, I would always regret my failure to face the challenge."

Bourassa left Shawinigan on December 31. Levesque had arranged a flight to Miami and had a vehicle ready so she could drive directly to the hotel at the Miami Lakes Country Club. She found out she was sharing a room with a female player from Texas, who told her to unpack her evening gown for a dinner party that was being hosted by the tournament sponsor.

It was then that Bourassa realized that she wouldn't have time to get homesick and that an exciting new chapter in her life was just beginning to unfold. After a few strenuous days of practice, the rookie pro was amazed to find a gallery of 40 Québeckers, all of them on vacation, ready to cheer her on as she teed off in her first event. Her brother Gilles had also made the trip.

She shot a 75 that day, which was good enough for 18th place in a field of 76 golfers. The second round didn't go as well, Bourassa ballooned to an 81 after three-putting on four holes. In the final round, her putting was back under control, and she closed with a 74. Her 230 total left Bourassa out of the money, but she finished in the top 80 percent of the field. In those days a rookie pro had to meet that requirement in three tournaments to earn a playing card.

Janie Blalok, the LPGA rookie of the year in 1971, was impressed by the Canadian's determination and maturity in her first tournament. "They say it takes five years to win on this tour, but I won in 15 months because, I believe, I was older—23—when I joined while most girls are 19 or 20. Jocelyne has the maturity as well as the necessary skills, as well as a lot of gumption."

Bourassa started her LPGA career with a compact, reliable swing. She was not one of the long hitters on the circuit, but by cutting down on her backswing (as suggested by her brother), Bourassa kept the ball in play.

It was obvious that putting was her main obstacle and that reading the greens on southern courses was a skill that needed some work. Bourassa took up billiards to improve her putting eye. "The game helps my eye coordination and visual perception. I suppose that measuring angles is common to both of them and it's helped."

In her first 20 starts, Bourassa finished in the top 10 in exactly half the events. In late August, she had a golden opportunity to win a title. On the last hole of the Southgate Ladies Open, Bourassa needed only a par to claim victory. When she misplayed her approach shot, the opportunity vanished; three putts on the green meant a playoff with Kathy Whitworth, the tour's best player and leading money winner.

The playoff was eerily similar to a situation Whitworth had found herself in four years earlier. In 1968, the Hall-of-Famer faced another Canadian rookie, Sandra Post, and lost in extra holes. However this time, Whitworth prevailed in the playoff. For five extra holes they battled, but when Bourassa gambled with a driver and landed behind a tree, she had to settle for second.

The younger players had been cheering for Bourassa, and when the playoff started, they gathered around the first tee to watch the duel. "I said to her, 'Is it all right if the three of us play against you?' and all she [Whitworth] could do was smile," recalled Bourassa. "I did not feel badly about losing the playoff, but I felt worse about losing on the last hole. There should have been no playoff."

The disappointment of letting a potential victory slip away didn't take away from what turned out to be a marvelous rookie season. Bourassa finished the 1972 campaign with over $16,000 in earnings while playing 23 events, the most money ever for a first year pro. She was named the LPGA rookie of the year and was recognized by her fellow golfers when she was voted the circuit's most colourful player.

Her bubbly personality and the uniqueness of her Québec accent brought Bourassa instant acceptance into the LPGA fraternity. The other pros called her "Frenchy," and the newspapers referred to her as "The French Girl."

As the year progressed, her English improved to the point where she found herself "thinking in English," which helped her communicate more clearly in interviews with the American media. Bourassa also managed to avoid the cliques that form on the tour; she was able to connect with almost all the players and develop close friendships.

She also discovered how tiring the grind of the LPGA season could become. In July she hit a low point and briefly contemplated quitting. "My attitude wasn't good, I was trying too hard, practicing too hard," recalled Bourassa, who finished 19th on the money list. "When I'm getting ready for a tournament, I became very aggressive and it wasn't good."

"But I also learned a lot about myself. I looked at how I finished in tournaments this year and discovered that I play in streaks—fifth, third, second, eighth and then 23rd. Tenth, fourth, eighth and then out of the money. I know now that if I play four or five tournaments in a row, I must take a week off if I want to continue to play well."

After finding success in her first professional season, Bourassa began to keep the promise she had made to her sponsor, Jean-Louis Levesque. She returned to Shawinigan in the off-season and conducted golfing clinics in her home province.

In late December, Bourassa received more recognition when Canada's sports editors selected her as Canada's Woman Athlete of the Year, and a poll of Canadian women's editors named her as Woman of the Year in Sport. Golf Canada also selected her as the country's Golf Personality of the Year.

In 1973, Bourassa completed the perfect ending to a script that had been started the year before by her benefactor Jean-Louis Levesque.

Inspired by the performance of the rookie pro, Levesque had announced during the 1972 season that he was willing to sponsor a Canadian LPGA event during an open week on the tour calendar the following June. Levesque had put together a syndicate that would offer a $50,000 purse (at that time the sixth largest in ladies golf).

The tournament would be played in Montreal and was named La Canadienne. It would be the first LPGA event held on Canadian soil. There was pressure on Bourassa to perform well before a hometown crowd that would at last get the opportunity to watch their favourite golfer in a professional tournament.

Despite temperatures below 15°C, Bourassa fired eight birdies in the first round, to shoot a 68 on the par-73 Municipal Golf Course. "I walked the 18 holes last night to be sure of the yardage on every hole," Bourassa told reporters after grabbing a two-stroke lead. "So this morning I wasn't particularly anxious about anything."

After the second round, the Canadian's lead shrank to one shot, after she fired an even-par 73. With Bourassa on the brink of winning on her home turf, the golf tournament became the number one sporting event in the province.

Thirty thousand spectators had attended over the preceding three days to watch the pro-am and the first two rounds. Another 12,000 fans showed up on the final day, most of them following Bourassa. The Montreal event set an all-time record for LPGA attendance.

And those spectators were treated to high sporting drama. The tournament became a three-player race between Bourassa and two Texans, Judy Rankin and Sandra Haynie. Rankin and Haynie completed the regulation 54 holes at five-under par, with Bourassa trailing by one shot with the final hole to play.

On the 18th green, the pride of Shawinigan needed to drain an 18-foot birdie putt to join the two Texans in a sudden-death playoff. With nerves of steel, Bourassa sank the testy putt, and the 12,000 Québeckers cheered with relief as their hometown favourite advanced to the playoff.

On the first extra hole, all three players made par on the 16th. Rankin was the first player to be eliminated when she bogeyed the par-3 17th. On the 18th, Bourassa gained the advantage when Haynie shanked her second shot into a pond. After the one-stroke penalty, the veteran from Fort Worth could only manage a bogey-six. Bourassa came home with a par and won her first LPGA event.

"I'm glad it happened at home," said a jubilant Bourassa after accepting the winning trophy and the $10,000 first prize. "I said Sunday I'd have to be super to win against these girls, and now that I've won, I just don't know what to say."

It was an amazing feat. Bourassa had triumphed in an event designed to showcase her talent; she somehow managed to push through all the expectations from her home fans to become the first and only Canadian woman to win an LPGA event on native soil.

The victory brought Bourassa into the spotlight, both in Canada and in the United States. She became a goodwill ambassador of the sport, with her charm and friendly presence; some reporters even dubbed Bourassa the Lee Trevino of woman's golf.

She was in high demand to attend pro-ams, clinics and sponsor dinners. Unlike the more glamorous LPGA pros, who were popular as much for their beauty as playing ability, Bourassa was comfortable exchanging banter and explaining the mechanics of the sport in an amusing, self-deprecating manner.

In 1973, Bourassa won almost $15,000 in official LPGA earnings, placing 34th on the money list. However, she stumbled a bit the following year with only one top-10 finish, earning $8000.

In 1975, she bounced back to play in 24 events and earned $26,518. She placed second in the Patty Burg tournament and finished 16th on the money list. It would be the last year she played a full schedule.

The grind of the previous four LPGA seasons caught up with Bourassa both physically and mentally. In 1976, she entered 15 events and won only $4000. She took six months off to set some new goals and plan the future.

"I needed a break mentally and physically," the 29-year-old told reporters. "I needed to come back home and live with my people to recharge my battery. That meant sacrificing number one, the tour, and I accepted that. If you want to be a top golfer, you have to exile yourself, you have to live 12 months of the year in the United States and stay in a warm climate and practice and be supervised by a coach."

Bourassa decided to make some changes to her schedule for 1977. She would only play the first nine months of the year and then go back to Québec through Christmas. She stayed true to her plan and entered 16 events. What she didn't foresee was a persistent soreness in her knees that grew worse as the golf season continued. Her best finish that year was 39th, and Bourassa made less than $900 in official earnings.

After the 1977 season ended, Bourassa had the first of two debilitating knee operations. In 1978, she managed to play only 12 events and had a best finish of 53rd. After another surgery in 1979 and more time away on rehab, she played in 13 tournaments and won only $908.61. Bourassa was still not healthy and had to decide whether to keep her playing career going.

"My last tour event was at the end of 1979. I was playing with pain, and I could not practice. I needed an operation, but I did not want to become a marginal player."

Bourassa was offered a job as golf coach at Arizona State, a job she enjoyed, but after one semester she accepted a position as the executive director of the du Maurier Classic. It was the opportunity to return home and to organize the LPGA event she had won (La Canadienne became the Peter Jackson Classic and then the du Maurier Classic) seven years earlier.

It was also a wonderful bit of irony; the rebel had become part of the golfing establishment. Bourassa remained in the position for 20 years, building the tournament into one of the LPGA's four major championships. Along the way she became an ambassador for Canadian women's golf, pioneering developmental programs for young women professionals that enabled them to work their way up to the LPGA.

When Bourassa started in 1980 there were only 20 Canadian women professionals. Ten years later, that number had jumped to 150.

"Jocelyne Bourassa has been an inspiration to every Canadian player," said Gail Graham, one of the next generation of golfers to have succeeded on the LPGA circuit. "She's done everything in the world for Canadian women."

In 2000, she resigned her position with the du Maurier Classic. One of her ambitions had been to support female golfers in her home province. At one time she had bought an 85-acre farm near Montreal with the goal of establishing a golf academy. Instead she went to work for Golf Québec to create a golf instruction program for the school curriculum.

Chapter Ten

Sandra Post
Our First Lady of Golf

Born Oakville, Ontario, 1948–

Who is Canada's best golfer of all-time? Golf aficionados would probably agree that Mike Weir is our top homegrown talent; others would say that George Knudson should be considered. But when you look at their records, a strong case can be made for a little spitfire of a player from Oakville, Ontario.

Sandra Post joined the LPGA Tour in 1968 and won a major, the LPGA Championship, in her first season. She was later named the tour's top rookie. Post went on to win eight LPGA events including back-to-back, Dinah Shore tournaments (the year after Post won her second title, the Dinah Shore was designated as a major championship). She won two more "unofficial" LPGA events, one in Australia and the second in Japan.

In 1979, Post was awarded the Lou Marsh Trophy as Canada's Athlete of the Year, the first golfer to ever have won the award. When she retired, Sandra Post was the seventh leading money winner in LPGA history.

So let's compare Weir vs. Post: one major title each, with Post adding two quasi majors with her Dinah Shore victories; eight tour wins each; highest finish on the money list goes to Post with second-place earnings in 1979, the best Weir has done was sixth in 2003; one Lou Marsh Trophy each; and in career earnings Post retired at seventh all-time, Weir is currently 11th.

Based on the importance of his Masters victory and the greater depth in men's golf, Weir deserves the nod as our best player, but Post's accomplishments in the sport should not be diminished. She is our best female golfer of all time.

Post grew up on a 25-acre fruit farm in Oakville and was introduced to golf at the age of five. While on a family vacation in Florida, her father, Cliff, took her to a tournament. At the event, she met Marilynn Smith (a founding member of the LPGA with 22 wins) who chatted with the youngster and gave her a ball, glove and some tees. On the way home she told her father that one day she would be a lady golfer. Her parents supported the dream and bought her a set of junior clubs.

"My parents always wanted me to be a professional golfer," she said years later. "Some parents want to send their kids to school; mine wanted me to play golf."

Her father was a good golfer, at one point competing in the Canadian Amateur, and was a member of the Oakville Golf and Country Club. Sandra began spending lots of time at the course, hitting balls whenever she had the chance. She took to the game with an abundance of passion and concentration; both would become trademarks throughout her golfing career.

In high school, Post joined the Trafalgar Golf Club and spent more time on the course than doing homework. Some days she would fit in 54 holes of golf, playing with some of the best junior male players in the province.

Post was totally devoted to the sport. Her parents took her to the United States in the winter to play in tournaments, and in the summer she competed in events at home. Post had her future mapped out, and it didn't include the social functions enjoyed by most teenagers.

"All I wanted to do was play golf. I didn't socialize," she says about her adolescence. "I didn't do a lot of social things around the country club. All I ever did was play golf and practice. I had one goal in mind—to join the ladies pro golf tour."

"I knew how good the competition was, and I knew what the juniors and amateurs were doing in the States. I knew if I was going to make in the U.S., I was going to have to work twice as hard. Coming from Canada, you're not going to get the same opportunity to become really, really good."

In 1964, she suffered her first major setback when she lost in the semi-finals of the Ontario Junior Girls Championship and was left off the provincial team that would compete for the Canadian Junior Championship in Calgary. A week later she took part in the Ontario Ladies' Amateur and shocked the golfing establishment in the province by winning the title in a sudden-death playoff.

Her victory put the Ontario golfing officials in a tough spot. Their new provincial champion had been left off the junior team. In the end, she was allowed to play as her parents put up the money for her to travel to Calgary. She repaid them by winning the championship by eight shots, overcoming the flu and a 104-degree fever.

Post went on to win both the Ontario and Canadian Junior Girls Championship in both 1965 and 1966. In March 1968, she paid a $50 entry fee and hit her first golf ball as a professional at a $10,000 tournament in Melbourne, Florida. She had become Canada's first woman golf pro.

The stocky, five-foot-four inch, brown-eyed blonde didn't make much of a splash in her first event, pocketing just $155 in finishing 26 shots behind the winner, Mickey Wright. In her third tournament, she won $1000 for a hole-in-one. Three months and eight tournaments later, she put herself in the golfing spotlight at the LPGA Championship in Sutton, Massachusetts.

Never worse than tied for the lead from the opening round, Post was deadlocked with the great Kathy Whitworth (winner of 88 pro tournaments) when they began a playoff round. It became a match play final, and Post, just removed as an amateur player, had a lot of experience with one-on-one competition. She was able to shelve any of the nervousness she should have felt.

The 20-year-old played flawlessly, shooting a 68 to Whitworth's 75. It was Post's day; on the 15th hole she played the shot of the tournament. After her tee shot just missed landing in a stream, Post played her recovery shot about a 100 feet from the pin. She was faced with a blind shot to the green. Using her trusty wedge, Post hit a high flopper that hit the edge of the green and rolled into the cup.

"I couldn't see anything, but when I heard the crowd, I knew it was in," she said after winning the $3000 top prize and a $1500 bonus from Spalding.

After the round, the vanquished Whitworth, who had played an exhibition match with Post when she was a 14-year-old, said, "To beat Sandra I probably would have had to play a career round. She was just great, and for one of her age, her poise is almost incredible. I predict she'll be one of our greatest players for a long, long time."

After the tournament, Post confidently told reporters that she had no weak points in her game. It was a bold statement, and she became known as a candid interview and usually charmed the media with her honest, yet perceptive comments about the game, her place in it and the life of a touring pro.

Post played in 26 events in her first season and finished in the top 10 in eight tournaments. The $17,835 she took home in prize money was the highest ever for a first-year player, and she easily won the Rookie of the Year award.

Canada's first female touring pro was also in demand as the LPGA's new glamour girl. She was paid $20,000 by Ford to travel across the country and play exhibitions in Canadian cities to promote the automakers new Ford Maverick.

A national women's clothing company and a golf magazine also signed her up.

Post followed up her rookie season by pocketing another $14,000 to finish 20th on the money list. She also became engaged to professional golfer Bob Elliot who at the time was just finishing up his army service in Vietnam.

"In the next two years I'm going to tend to business and golf and then quit the tour and get married," predicted Post.

In 1970 she did marry Elliot. They seemed well matched; both were extroverts who liked to have fun. The relationship, however, was full of ups and downs. The attention required by Post to keep the marriage working meant that she neglected her golf game. Her earnings dwindled to just $2400, and she failed to make the top 10 in any of the events she entered. In 1971 things didn't get any better.

The marriage became even more strained when Elliot failed to find a place on the PGA Tour. Even a try in Canada failed when he was reprimanded for a rules violation at the Manitoba Open. The strain of their careers led them to divorce in 1972.

"Maybe I just got married too soon," Post said about the troubled marriage. "Maybe we just were not cut out for each other and didn't know it. I don't know."

"When I was on tour I felt I should be home. At home, I wanted to be playing. We were always going down the road in opposite directions."

Post was left trying to revive a golfing career that had hit rock bottom. After the divorce, she didn't pick up a club for five months. In the 39 tournaments she had played while coping with her domestic woes, Post had won less than $12,000. After her brief vacation she once again rededicated her energy to reaching the top echelons of the sport.

At the age of 24, Post began her comeback. In 1973, she became a full-time golfer again and won $12,000 in her first 12 starts. Things went even better the next year. Post had four third-place finishes on the regular LPGA Tour and then won the Far East event in Melbourne, her first victory in six years. The tournament was not an LPGA sanctioned event, but the $13,000 first place prize money attracted all the top players.

"You can just imagine how good it is to win. The money is great, but to win a tournament after four thirds this year is really something," said Post, who burst into tears after sinking the winning putt.

Post finished the 1974 season with $50,000 in official Tour winnings, good enough for 15th place. "I got my determination back, and I started working really hard," said Post about her comeback. "And

I gained a lot of confidence. I believe in my ability now. That's the important thing."

She was also back as one of the sport's glamour girls. Along with players like Laura Baugh, Jan Stephenson and Renee Powell, Post helped to raise the LPGA's profile through the 1970s. Mixing sex appeal with athletic wholesomeness, Post helped to sell a sport that had little money for marketing.

"We all played for the love of the game, first of all. And love of the sport," said Post about the growth of the women's tour. "And we were also promoting women in sport and women. There were a lot of women issues involved in the '60s and the '70s and the '80s and it was a very exciting time for the LPGA Tour."

"I came along at the best of times. The '70s were golden. We were considered interesting, even amazing. Television came on board, money came on board. It was glamorous."

And it was a tough grind. Post played 28 tour events each year. Throw in the unofficial tournaments, often on other continents, plus the commitments to sponsors and Post was on the road for 11 months of the year, getting home for only a total of about seven weeks during that period.

Unlike some of the tour regulars who combined partying with playing golf, Post lived a structured life on the road. "I never even go to bars," said Post about her schedule. "I need at least eight hours sleep every night, and you have to watch those things. You can't just think about how you'll feel this week, you have to think of the next 40 weeks."

Post was one of the more popular players on the circuit; her sense of optimism and determination made her a true professional. Her quick smile and engaging manner on the golf course was in sharp contrast to many of the pros determined to maintain their "game face" throughout a tournament.

The one thing that was missing in Post's comeback was an official LPGA victory. In 1977 she had banked $77,727 in earnings, the ninth best on the tour, but not since her rookie year had the Canadian been at the top of the leaderboard after the final hole of a tourney. She did have 10 second-place finishes through the drought, but it wasn't until April 1978 that she was able to break through, whipping Australian Penny Pulz in a playoff to take the first prize of $36,000 in the $240,000 Dinah Shore tournament.

Four months later she defeated her old rival, Kathy Whitworth, in another playoff to win $22,500 at the Lady Stroh's Open in Detroit. After nine years without a victory, Post was able to win the two richest tournaments in women's golf in less than six months.

"There were times when I got down," admitted Post about her long absence as a tournament winner. "But I was sure I could win again."

With a new sense of confidence, Post followed up 1978 with a career season. She started things off by defending her title at the Dinah Shore Winners Circle, then added the Lady Michelob title and the ERA Real Estate Classic Championship. She had an amazing 16 top-10 finishes.

Post finished second to Nancy Lopez in LPGA earnings, with $178,750; at that time the most money ever won by Canadian golfer, man or woman, in a single season. She also placed third in scoring average at 72.30 strokes per round, behind Lopez and Jane Blalock.

It was a storybook season, culminating in Post being selected as Canada's Athlete of the Year (Lou Marsh Trophy), Woman Athlete of the Year (Bobby Rosenfeld Award), Tee Off Magazine Golfer of the Year and Ontario Athlete of the Year.

"It was especially gratifying when I knew I was being considered for the Rosenfeld Award as top woman," Post said about the recognition at the end of the year. "I hadn't won any awards from my province or my country, and to think that I had just put in a tremendous season, and it might not be enough...well it was something I had to cope with."

"When I got a call the next day to tell me I had won the Lou Marsh Trophy as well, I was amazed. It hadn't even entered my mind. What chance did a golfer have for selection against hockey in this country?"

Post, in fact, was the first golfer to ever win the Lou Marsh, outpolling racing car driver Gilles Villeneuve. Despite living in Florida for over a decade, Post made it clear that she still considered Oakville her home.

"I live in Florida," Post said, "but I am Canadian, staunchly Canadian. I hold a Canadian passport and will continue to do so. I'll never give up my Canadian citizenship."

"I've felt that people in Canada think I've abandoned the country. I never did. I just want to be the best in the entire world. That's why I moved to Florida."

In 1979, Post pushed herself to be the best player she could be: "I made the commitment that I would work as hard as I possibly could to see what I really could do on tour. I decided to lay it on the line, and after it was all over I was drained."

Still, Post managed to win the West Virginia Classic in 1980 and added another $102,822 to her career earnings. In 1981, she won her eighth and final LPGA event, the McDonald's Kid Classic and $71,191 for the year.

The grind of the professional golfing life started to catch up with the veteran player. It wasn't as much fun anymore. Post had to force herself to go to the practice range and push herself through the LPGA season. Her passion for the pro life was starting to wane. In 1982, she won only $22,383.

The next year, she played a full schedule through the first half of the season, 16 events in total, and won only $24,726. At a tournament in Atlanta, she pushed herself to give the kind of effort that had been automatic just a few years earlier. It worked in that Post finished second, pocketing $14,700, but along the way, she lost feeling in her right thumb.

Despite extensive testing, doctors couldn't find a physical problem. She took six weeks off, going home to Oakville to visit family and friends. Over the break, Post decided she was through as a full-time LPGA professional.

At the age of 35, with almost $750,000 in career earnings accumulated over 16 seasons, Post was ready to move on to a new challenge. Not surprisingly, golf remained the centre of her post-playing career. She poured her considerable energy into teaching, starting the Sandra Post Golf School. Post also became a golf analyst for CTV television, working Canadian events such as the du Maurier Classic.

In 1998, she became the Executive Editor of *World of Women's Golf* magazine. She became a tireless advocate for women's golf, describing her mission as, "How do we make the game easier for women to play?"

Post also co-wrote a book in 1998 entitled *Sandra Post and Me* with Loral Dean. It described the journey the two middle-aged women took together—Post the teacher, Dean the pupil. It was a candid accounting of the ups and downs of a woman learning a new sport at an advanced age.

Throw in her role as an equipment designer, and Canada's first LPGA professional has had an amazing ride in the sport for over 40 years. At a 2005 press conference in Calgary where she was promoting her latest line of women's clubs, Post summed up her time after leaving the LPGA Tour.

"If you'd have told me then that 41 years later I'd have my name on a line of clubs and more passion than ever over this game and about the welfare of women golfers in this country, I'd have said you're not a well person."

"I'm really happy where I am. I take all my knowledge, all my experience, my record and I bring it to the table in a very good sport."

Chapter Eleven

George Knudson
The Natural Swinger

Born Winnipeg, Manitoba, 1937–1989

George Knudson once said that playing great golf is an art, just as painting or writing is an art. If that description is accurate, then Knudson was certainly an artist. His entire life was devoted to finding and then teaching the perfect swing. Through countless hours of theorizing and practice, he became what other golfers called a "pure swinger." Jack Nicklaus once said Knudson had a million-dollar swing, other golfers said he swung the club better than anybody since Ben Hogan. The great Hogan himself said that Knudson had the best swing of his generation.

His legacy as a Canadian golfer was unmatched when he passed away in 1989. Winner of eight PGA events and over $500,000 in Tour earnings, he retired from the circuit as one of the top-50 money winners of all-time. Until Mike Weir came along, Knudson was the standard for what young Canadian golfers hoped to achieve.

He was born in Winnipeg in 1937 and took up the game as a teenager. Golf quickly became a passion; he would start playing so early in the spring and play so late into the fall that he had to wear rubber boots just to navigate the mud.

Knudson went to work at the St. Charles Club in Winnipeg, cleaning and repairing clubs. He chose to work in the locker room instead of the pro shop because it was easier to sneak out to the driving range to work on his own game. He practiced putting after dark by shining the headlights of his car on the green.

Even as an amateur, Knudson became a local legend for his shot-making talents. "I was his caddy for a couple of years," recalled Gerry Chatelaine, who grew up in Winnipeg and later became a club pro. "He was the easiest golfer I ever shagged balls for. He'd tell me to go out there 150 yards for seven-iron shots. I never had to take two steps either way from where he told me to stand, and I'd catch the balls with my cap. He'd then wave me back 10 or 15 yards and do the same with the six-iron. He was amazing, even then as an amateur."

In 1954, he won the Manitoba Junior Championship, defended the title the next year and added the Canadian Junior Championship to his early winnings. In 1958, he turned professional. He was just 21 and had moved to Toronto to become an assistant professional, teaching golf at a local course.

Two years earlier, shortly after leaving high school Knudson hitched a ride to Pebble Beach, California to watch his idol Ben Hogan play at Cypress Point in a foursome with Jimmy Demaret, Bing Crosby and Bob Hope as part of the Bing Crosby National Pro-Am.

He caught up to Hogan on the 14th hole and watched him put his second shot about six feet from the hole. "It all started with that shot. I was quickly hooked on the way Hogan went about being a golfer."

"From that day on, I took every opportunity I had to watch Hogan. I'd drop my clubs and observe him. I knew I could learn a lot just sitting there quietly. I was watching the maestro. He made it look so routine all the time."

"When he set up over the ball, he knew the shot was going to come off. You knew it. Everybody knew it. And I wanted the same feeling, the same certainty."

The next year, when he was still an amateur, he caddied the PGA winter tour for Al Balding and Stan Leonard and learned how professionals played the game. He sat on a golf bag on the practice range at tournaments and watched how Hogan dedicated himself to the craft.

In 1958, Knudson was recognized as Canada's next best hope for the PGA Tour. He had developed a marvellously fluid and textbook swing. That summer during the British and American Motors Bursary Tournament in Toronto, the top three players qualified for the PGA winter tour. Knudson and Moe Norman, then the top amateur in Canada (more about Moe in Chapter 14) were among the leaders heading into the final round.

The two Canadians were not close friends, but they were usually cordial and friendly with each other. On this morning, however, Knudson's competitive nature took over.

The lanky youngster wouldn't even look at Norman as they prepared to head out in the final group. On the first hole, a short but sharp dogleg left with a creek running in front of the green and out-of-bounds guarding the left side, Knudson surprised his opponent and the gallery by pulling out a driver.

Knudson then turned around, looked at Norman and said, "Just watch me. Watch the way golf should really be played." With that he nailed a perfect drive over the creek and trees and landed his ball on the green. Knudson two-putted for the birdie and went on to defeat his rival by seven strokes.

In winning the tournament, Knudson qualified for the PGA Tour (Norman also made it). At last he would get to test himself against the world's best players. He started his journey to the U.S. in a new car, with the $1500 he'd won at the Bursary in his pocket.

Knudson stopped in Las Vegas, and since he had a gambling itch, he decided to take a few hours to scratch it at a blackjack table. After a couple of hot hands, he had built up his bankroll to $4000. The youngster decided not to push his luck and headed out of town. Just as he escaped the alluring tentacles of Vegas, he ran his car into a cement abutment on a bridge, demolishing his new ride while somehow escaping injury.

To make things worse, Knudson decided to go back to the blackjack table to recoup the funds required to replace his written-off vehicle. Within a few hours he had lost all his money. He even had to borrow a dime just to call his father back in Winnipeg to tell him the news.

The elder Knudson was surprisingly sympathetic and borrowed $1500 for his son to get started on the PGA Tour. It took a while for Knudson to earn enough money to pay his Dad back.

Gambling was not Knudson's only vice. In a profile in *Maclean's* magazine, he said he would finish a round of golf with a couple of beers, then perhaps a few vodka martinis. His favourite beverage was Chivas Regal on the rocks, which he enjoyed after a tournament ended. Like many professional golfers of his era, Knudson was also a chain smoker, an addiction he couldn't shake for over 30 years.

Conversely, Knudson was perhaps the fittest player on the Tour. In an era long before Tiger Woods showed the golfing establishment the benefits of strength training, Knudson followed a program designed by Lloyd Percival, a Toronto fitness guru. Knudson weighed only 135 pounds and couldn't play more than a couple of weeks in a row without becoming physically and emotionally depleted. Two years following Percival's training program, and Knudson was up to 172 pounds, working out with weights, doing isometrics and running.

"George did everything to excess, weight lifting or drinking," said one his closest friends, Jack McLaughlin, who asked Knudson to develop a teaching program for talented Canadian golfers. "But he kept in great shape, which allowed him the luxury of smoking."

For the next three years, Knudson made almost all of his money in Canada. In three PGA seasons he cashed only one cheque—$100 for making the cut at the Crosby. In 1960 Knudson had a breakthrough in his understanding of his swing. He described his epiphany as figuring out the golf swing had to be "impersonal" to work.

His analysis of the golf swing was often so technical and "way-out" as Canadian golfing legend Stan Leonard described his approach, that most of his peers couldn't follow his theories. His personal breakthrough, however, was very real, and his new confidence in his abilities paid off in 1961, when he won the Coral Gables Open, his first PGA victory.

He followed up his Coral Gables victory with the Portland Open Championship in 1963, and a year later he won the Fresno Open. Knudson had become comfortable on the PGA Tour, but he developed a reputation as a tightly wound loner who didn't relate well to the fans who came out to watch.

He was an odd sight on the golf course, often hiding behind his trademark dark sunglasses, and for some reason he liked to wear a grey cardigan on hot days. His wardrobe was colourless—black, white and grey dominated. Cigarette in hand, he often shuffled down the golf course as if he could he fall over at any moment. Knudson projected an attitude of detached coolness.

When asked why he didn't play up to the galleries, he didn't hold much back in his response, "Look, they applaud scores. They applaud leaders. But they don't know or appreciate a good golf shot. Hogan knows that. I know that. They clap and yell like hell for a shot that might have been the worst the golfer hit all day. I'm sorry, I can't respect a gallery."

It wasn't until he was retired from competitive golf that Knudson tried to communicate to golf fans what really drove him to play the game. Making money, of course, was important; he had a young family to support (his wife Shirley and three sons). But Knudson's quest to develop a reliable, natural golf swing was what kept him devoted to the sport.

In 1966, he hit what he later called, his perfect shot. It came during the third round of the World Cup in Spain. Playing from a valley to an elevated green, Knudson hit the ball 180 yards to within a few feet from the hole. "I still don't know how it didn't go in." He had visualized exactly what he wanted to do and executed the shot to perfection. It was almost inconsequential that he was the individual scoring champion in the team event.

In 1967, Knudson was paired against Jack Nicklaus in the final round of the Greater New Orleans Open. At the end of the afternoon it was the one-time Winnipeg caddie who ended up with the $20,000 first-place cheque. Reporters covering Knudson were amazed that he held on for the win. Never one to wear golf gloves, his hands were red and raw from overdoing it at practice sessions during the week, but still he beat the field.

In 1968, Knudson won the Phoenix and Tucson Opens in consecutive weeks. "I really don't think I could have made better golf swings than during those seven weeks. The fact is that I could have won five out of the seven tournaments if I'd made some putts. That's how well I was playing."

In winning the Phoenix Open, Knudson knew he had reached a new level of success. "I was absolutely knocking the flag down, stuffing it down the throat every hole. The game was very easy, and it stayed easy. Even though I didn't get much sleep the night before the last round— I had a one-shot lead, and would rather have been a shot or two behind—I still had enough strength to go on and win. That was gratifying. My endurance program seemed to be paying off."

At Tucson, Knudson was four strokes back of the leader heading into the final round. He figured a 66 would get him into a playoff, and heading to the 10th tee, he told his caddy that if he shot a 32 on the back nine it would be enough. He ended up shooting a 31 and won outright.

"On the 18th, a 465-yard par four, I hit driver, six-iron. The other guys were coming in with four-woods and long irons. I must have carried that last drive 280 yards, and the hole is a dynamic driving hole; water left and right with a camelback fairway. Miss the ball just a bit, and it's in the water. But I nailed the drive, knocked the iron on the green, two-putted and won."

Instead of being elated at winning two tournaments in a row, Knudson was done in. He had pushed himself to his emotional and physical limit. In trying to control his emotional side so rigidly, he had totally worn himself out. He still hadn't mastered the ability to relax on the golf course.

When Knudson returned to Toronto after winning both tournaments, there was a civic reception and messages of congratulations from across the country waiting for him. But he still felt the stress of the previous seven weeks. He missed the cut at the Doral Open in Miami when he returned to the Tour and then played only sporadically the rest of the year.

In 1969, Knudson showed his mettle when during the final round of the Wills Masters Golf event in Melbourne, he collapsed on the fourth hole, complaining of shortness of breath and fever. Knudson was winning the tournament by three strokes and refused to withdraw. After a short break where a doctor have him glucose-enriched water and salt tablets, the Canadian pro continued for the rest of the round.

The doctor was also able to convince him to shed his heavy sweater for the remaining holes, and with the tournament director shading him with an umbrella, Knudson held on to win by two strokes. "I don't think I ever felt worse during a tournament," he said later. "I thought I was going to faint on the fourth, and I seriously considered pulling out."

The same year, Knudson came close to winning the Masters. In the final round, he was right in the thick of things, but his putter let him down. He ended up tied for second with Billie Casper and Tom Weiskopf, one stroke behind winner George Archer.

In 1972, he won the Kaiser International Open in Napa, California. It was the first time he felt joy, instead of relief after winning. For once he was able to take pleasure in the competitive environment of tournament golf. He said later it was the last time he captured that feeling again on the Tour.

In the mid-'70s, Knudson battled a chronic back condition that forced him to miss much of the Tour schedule for three seasons. He had become a part-time player and began looking for something else to replace his nomadic PGA life. His three sons had also reached school age, and he missed them too much to devote himself to the travel required to earn a living as a pro golfer.

He began a gradual re-shifting of his priorities to start teaching the game full-time.

In looking back at Knudson's record over the years, Lee Trevino said the Canadian would have won a lot more PGA events if he had worked on his putting. Knudson admitted to never liking that aspect of the game, so he never bothered to practice.

By the mid-1980s, he was totally devoted to teaching at his golf school near Toronto. He had evolved from being a tightly wound, stiff golfer to one advocating a natural, relaxed swing. He even applied the same principal to putting, the one facet of the game that had given him so much trouble.

In June 1987, doctors discovered a cancerous spot on his lung, and he began treatment immediately. Knudson had just finished up a seminar series that sent him touring throughout the country, and he was preparing to publish an instruction manual for professional golfers. Over the next year, he battled the disease, and just after turning 50, he was told the cancer was in remission.

He never complained about the chemotherapy and radiation treatments that sapped much of his energy. He had smoked heavily for three decades, a habit he wasn't able to shake. "Hey, I smoked those things," he said. "Who was I to think that cancer wouldn't get me?"

Over the summer of 1988, the cancer returned and began to spread throughout his body. He entered the hospital in November, and despite the pain and effects of medication he worked on another instructional video and authored a book with Lorne Rubenstein entitled *The Natural Golf Swing*. He went on another cross-country trip to promote the book, a tour that allowed his many fans across Canada to pay tribute to his amazing golf career.

In his book, he puts forth a theory that golf is a game of motion directed toward a target. The ball just gets in the way of the motion. He once shot a 67 at Glenn Abbey, one of the homes of the Canadian Open, while closing his eyes on each swing. Knudson said many blind people could play golf well because they're not concerned about the ball, once they are lined up towards the target; the ball itself is irrelevant.

The book was a wonderful legacy. The results of the hours Knudson spent learning and mastering the mechanics of the game were passed on to other generations. He wanted golfers to enjoy the game and not over-analyze their swings.

Over his 20-year professional career, Knudson didn't receive the accolades that he might have deserved as Canada's best golfer. But even as Knudson quietly went about his business, his fellow pros appreciated the talent and dedication he brought to his craft.

"The players respected George," said fellow touring pro Art Wall in an interview with Lorne Rubenstein. "They knew how great he was. That's not a word we use too much, but it applies in his case. I'm not sure that Canadians realize how talented he was. But the players on tour knew. That's what counts."

In January 1989, Knudson succumbed to lung cancer at the age of 51. In one chapter of his book, Knudson takes the reader on a little sidebar, away from the technical side of the swing to describe the beauty of the game of golf on his favourite course, Cypress Point at Pebble Beach.

"If I had one round left in my life, I'd play Cypress at 7:15 in the morning when the fog was still in. I can still see the setting on the first tee. The fog is so thick that I can't see the cypress tree that's down there 240 yards on the right side, but I know it's there. As I walk down the hill to my second shot, I'm looking up through the fog, and I can see the sunlight and the green. I'm in heaven. And it never lets up until you get to the clubhouse. This is the kind of place where I first saw Ben Hogan."

Chapter Twelve

Stan Leonard
The Oldest Rookie

Born Sarnia, Ontario, 1970–

Sometimes success comes late in life. At the age of 40, when most professional golfers are thinking of the Seniors Tour beckoning a decade down the road, Stan Leonard decided to leave his comfortable job as head pro at the beautiful Marine Drive Golf Club in Vancouver to head south and give the PGA Tour a real try.

"It was a difficult decision," said Leonard about his life-changing choice. "But it was the decision that had to be made. I'd tested the Tour from time to time, and I felt I could compete with the best of them, with Hogan and Nelson and Snead and the others. Even in those days a 40-year-old was old by athletic standards. But I felt fit physically and mentally."

Leonard took on the big boys in the States after dominating the golf scene in Canada for over 20 years. He won 40 Canadian titles, including eight Canadian PGA Championships and five runner-up finishes. He also captured nine Alberta Opens, five BC Opens, two Saskatchewan Opens, a couple of Canadian Match Play titles and was the best Canadian pro at eight Canadian Opens.

For over 10 years, Leonard had been the resident pro at Marine Drive. In 1955, he decided it was time to measure his skills against the best players in the world. He was at the peak of his game, a long hitter, a great iron player and a streaky putter who could sink the long ones with the best of them.

Before heading to the United States, Leonard had played well in two major events outside the PGA Tour. In 1951 at the Canadian Open in Montréal he held the lead after 36 holes and was tied for first after 54. With three holes to play in the final round, he was still tied for the lead, but on the 16th, he lofted a tee shot behind a tool shed. He would bogey the hole and fall out of contention.

Two years later, Leonard showed Canadian fans that he could handle the pressure of a big tournament when he won the individual title at the World Cup (then an important event that drew the best players from around the globe). With a Canadian crowd cheering him on (the event was held in Montréal), Stan the Man, as his fans called him, held off a deep and talented field to win top honours.

━ ━

Leonard was born in Vancouver in 1915. He grew up in a blue-collar neighbourhood on the east side of the city. He was a scrappy, spunky kind of kid who never backed down from anyone. He took on bullies and ignored the authority figures in his life when he thought their discipline was unfair. His fiery temperament propelled him through many of life's obstacles, but in his later years he admitted that it delayed his development as a golfer.

There wasn't much in the way of extra money in the Leonard household. When he discovered the game at the age of nine, his first club was a hickory shaft and his first golf balls were rocks. Leonard's driving range was the laneway and his shots often sailed off the fairway. "There were houses on both sides of that lane, and I didn't know what I was doing," remembered Leonard in a 2005 profile in the *Vancouver Sun*. "I remember them bouncing off houses, and it wasn't too long before the police were called."

Leonard and his friends all caddied at a course called Shaughnessy Heights. For 50 cents a bag he would caddy through the afternoon and then hop the fence in the early evening to play a few holes with his friends.

"We'd caddy at Shaughnessy, and we used to find the odd golf ball," Leonard said. "Part of the course was on the other side of Oak Street, and we used to hop the fence and play four or five holes. We used to get kicked off there every night. That's where I really learned to play golf. That's where it all began."

Leonard's older brother Bill was a partner in a golf club manufacturing business with a pro named Dave McLeod. Bill was also a fine amateur golfer and became a club pro at the Calgary Country Club during the mid-1930s. Stan was hired to make clubs in McLeod's golf factory (the company went through several name changes before settling on "Titleist"). McLeod also took the aspiring youngster under his wing to teach him some of the basics of the game.

Leonard's short fuse was always near the surface. When things weren't going well on the golf course, he threw his clubs and had temper tantrums. His inelegant swing resulted in some savage hooks, but despite his short stature (five-feet, nine-inches and 160 pounds), Leonard was known as one of the longest hitters in the province.

In 1932, at the age of 17, Leonard won his first BC Amateur title using a set of clubs he had made for himself. It was the start of a run that saw him juggle competitive play with club pro positions in the Lower Mainland. For the next 20 years he became a legend on the West Coast as he won almost every Western Canadian event while landing the head pro position at Marine Drive just as World War II ended.

Leonard was described as the pro with Popeye arms, and most of his attention was focused on bashing the ball farther than anyone else. In one Vancouver-area tournament, he was encouraged to out-hit an opponent from Hollywood who was renowned for his smashing drives. Leonard astounded everyone by outdistancing the American by 25 yards. On the fourth tee, the puny Canadian launched one 345 yards, and on the 11th, he nailed his drive 352 yards.

In his early tournament days Leonard battled two deficiencies in his golf game. He was a long hitter but had a tendency to hit wicked hooks off the tee. "My big weakness was control off the tee," Leonard confirmed. "I could hit it a mile, but my control was often bad."

"There wasn't a better club thrower around," said Leonard about his temper. "A lot of folks tried to correct that, yet I believe my temper helped make me a better player. It kept me fighting mad. Being angry, I could never get complacent."

His tough, determined attitude worked to his advantage in tournament play. "You have to have a little meanness in you to win," Leonard would say, but he also let his hot temperament impact his effectiveness when things weren't going well.

By the time he left Vancouver to give the PGA a try, Leonard had become a polished player. He changed his grip, sacrificing some power, but adding much more accuracy to his drives. Others admired his swing for its fluidity, and his temper finally found the perfect outlet.

"I guess I stopped acting up as my game matured," said Leonard in an excerpt from Arv Olson's book, *Backspin: 100 years of Golf in British Columbia*. "My guiding light was my brother, though it took quite some time to see how Bill kept things in proper perspective. I was always flying off the handle for one reason or another, and it got me into some trouble."

While he was club pro at Marine Drive, Leonard would head south in January to play five or six weeks of the winter tour in California and Arizona, measuring himself against American competition. On the 1954 winter tour, he shot a course record 63 at the Phoenix Open and finished only three shots behind the winner. A few weeks later, he finished fourth at the Crosby tournament.

With more invitations to play events in the States, Leonard decided it was time to become a full-time Tour player. "A lot of people, including some of my own members, thought I was crazy, thinking I could go down there at my age and make a living. I was putting all the chips on the table. I still had to buy groceries for my wife and daughter, and I had a mortgage. But I couldn't rest until I tried it, and I knew time was wasting. My only regret is that I didn't do it five or six years earlier."

In his 1955 debut, Leonard finished eighth at the San Diego Open, making $513. He earned a payday in nine of his 10 starts and finished fourth in the Canadian Open that year. In the off-season, Leonard broke his foot while repairing his roof, but in 1956, he still managed to earn money in 12 of 13 tournaments. His total earnings for the year were $8831, good enough for 33rd on the money list.

In 1957, he won his first title, a three-shot victory at the Greater Greensboro Open. Not only did he win $2000, but at the age of 42, he also proved that he was good enough to play against the best players in the world. Late in the season he won an extra $2500 by scoring one of his 11 career holes-in-one during the Western Open.

Leonard attributed his success to playing each round with purpose and a plan of action. Off the tee he remained committed to sacrificing distance for accuracy. He went to lighter woods and took to heart Ben Hogan's revelation that he had developed a fade to counteract his problem hook off the tee. Leonard adjusted his swing to hit left-to-right fades that found the fairway on almost every shot. Stan the Man became a consistent golfer. At one stretch starting in 1959, he made the cut in 32 straight tournaments, which set a PGA record. In those days even if you made the cut, it didn't guarantee a paycheque.

"If you won 1000 bucks in a week, you had a good week," said Leonard in a 1983 interview. "Of course things were different. We went by car, maybe a day's drive, maybe two, a thousand miles sometimes. Now all tournaments have a central hotel, and everything is laid out for the players. We used to drive around and find a cheap motel. One of the guys would say, 'Hey, there's one down the street for $10, and we'd all go there.'"

"It is much more competitive now, but once you are in the field, it is easier to make a living. Now everyone who makes the cut gets a cheque. It used to be maybe just 25 to 30 golfers."

By winning the Greater Greensboro Open, Leonard received an invitation to play in the 1958 Tournament of Champions tournament in Las Vegas, one of the richest events on the

Tour. He took full advantage of the opportunity, picking up his second tour victory and the first place loot of $10,000 (presented to him in 10,000 silver dollars). Leonard joked that win was like "winning a million bucks today."

The Canadian actually doubled his money that week. After accepting the championship trophy and returning to his hotel room, Leonard received a phone call from a stranger telling him he had a gift.

"I went up to this guy's room at the Desert Inn and he handed me a cheque for 10 grand," Leonard recalled years later. The benevolent stranger had placed a large bet on Stan the Man. "He said, 'I didn't know you from a bar of soap.' I said, 'Is this any good?' and he says, 'Certainly, you go to the bank tomorrow and cash it; it's okay.' Sure enough it was."

In total, Leonard earned $22,827 in only 15 Tour starts (Arnold Palmer was the top money earner with $42,607), and the Canadian was among the leaders in the competition for the Vardon Trophy (awarded each year to the PGA Tour's leader in scoring average). Leonard averaged 70.8 strokes in the 58 rounds he played. He finished off the year with a fifth-place finish at the Canadian Open, taking home an extra $1800.

In 1959, Leonard made the cut in 12 of 13 events, but he made only $6767, an amount that didn't even cover his expenses. The year was saved when he won his second individual championship at the World Cup in Melbourne, defeating Peter Thomson in a playoff. The Metropolitan Golfers Writers of America named him player of the year, and the Greater Vancouver Tourist Board honoured him as the city's Goodwill Ambassador for the year.

In 1960, Leonard won his last PGA event with a victory at the Western Open. The $5000 cheque pushed his earnings that year to $14,141 in 16 starts.

"When I won at Greensboro, it made me feel like I belonged out there," summed up Leonard. "But winning the Tournament of Champions was one of the biggest highlights of my career. The Western Open victory came right out of the blue because I hadn't been playing well before that."

Over the next few seasons, Leonard became less of a factor on the Tour. Nerves crept into his game; the snap hooks returned, and his putting was jittery. In 1964, he made only $5200. By 1967, he left the PGA Tour, playing just a few Canadian tournaments until 1971, when he retired from competitive golf.

Despite the three Tour victories and winning over 40 Canadian titles, Leonard is best remembered for his success at the Masters. He played golf's most prestigious event 12 times, and for three years running (1958, '59 and '60), Leonard had a legitimate chance to win at Augusta. Altogether he recorded four top-10 finishes in his dozen appearances and only missed the cut three times.

The course at Augusta National was well suited to his game. He drove the ball right to left, which is required on at least a half dozen holes. The key to scoring at Augusta is being able to place the ball in the right spots in the fairway to attack the greens, and the Canadian was known as a shot maker. And if Leonard was on one of his putting streaks, he could handle the treacherous greens.

"They are the most difficult greens I think I've ever seen," said Leonard about his favourite course. "They're big, they're rolling, and they're so damned fast you wouldn't believe it."

In 1959, Leonard had his best chance to win the title. Heading into the final round, Leonard shared the lead with the great Arnold Palmer. Fans across the country fortunate enough to own television sets tuned in, and others stayed close to their radios to see and hear if Leonard could win the green jacket.

In Vancouver, coverage of Leonard's bid to become Canada's first major champion was low key. Neither one of the two daily newspapers sent a reporter, they instead relied on wire service stories. There was no Sunday edition of either daily so many people in the city didn't even know that their favourite golfing son was in contention.

On the final day of the tourney, Art Wall Jr. came from six strokes back to shoot a 66 and win the title by a single stroke over Cary Middlecoff. Palmer shot a 74 to finish third. Leonard's 75 was good for fourth. Stan the Man was paired with Middlecoff in the final round, a bit of bad luck in that Middlecoff was a notoriously slow player, while Leonard liked to play fast.

"I remember some of the players coming up to me and saying 'Look Leonard, you've got Middlecoff tomorrow, don't let it bother you.' I guess I did let it work on me," recalled Leonard almost 40 years later in a *Vancouver Sun* interview. " I played like a dog, shot 75 and let three or four guys pass me."

Leonard actually started well during the final round, but he fell out of contention at the notorious Amen Corner, bogeying the 11th, 12th and 13th holes. For his fourth-place finish he earned $2625. After the tournament, he received a letter from Clifford Roberts, the legendary Masters chairman. The letter complemented Leonard on his fine play, and Roberts added: "I think Cary Middlecoff cost you the tournament."

Leonard also finished fourth at Augusta in 1958, shooting a final round 71 to end up two shots back of Palmer. In 1960 he was ninth. In his 12 appearances at the Masters, stretching between 1952 and 1965, he took home $12,902, not a bad total considering the size of the purses in those days.

By 1967, Stan the Man had grown tired of the PGA grind. To keep his nerves in check, he had been a two-pack-a-day smoker for 30 years, but even his strong Buckingham cigarettes were unable to keep his putting jitters at bay. And life on the Tour had burned him out.

"The pros who go by plane these days have no idea what it's like to drive for days on end to get to the tee on time. It was nothing for me to drive 800 miles straight to reach the site of the next tournament. No golfer can be at his best in these circumstances. I often wonder how men like Hogan and Snead and Nelson came through as great as they did in the early days."

After wrapping things up as a tour pro, Leonard became a golf consultant and designed and built courses for a few years. He also did a stint on CBC television as a colour commentator for some of the bigger tournaments.

In 1974, he became Director of Golf at the Desert Island Country Club in Palm Springs, a position he held for over a decade, while still living four months of the year in Vancouver. Leonard played a few Legends of Golf tournaments in the 1980s, but he wasn't able to adjust to competitive play again. "I found my nerves were as bad as ever, worse than I expected."

Leonard remained at Desert Island, teaching golf, until 1991. In his later years, he suffered from vertigo, which prevented him from swinging a club. In 2005, at the age of 90, Leonard died from a heart attack.

A celebration of his life was held at his beloved Marine Drive course in Vancouver. Tributes poured in from across the country. Richard Zokol, a Marine Drive member, commented that legends like Leonard paved the way for the next generation of professional golfers on the West Coast who found success on the PGA Tour. "We have to build on that legendary status and pass it along to future players."

Chapter Thirteen

Al Balding
Canada's Forgotten Champion

Born Toronto, Ontario, 1924–2006

When you rub people the wrong way, sometimes it can come back to bite you. Al Balding could be gruff and brutally honest, but he was also the first Canadian player to ever win a PGA event.

He was once the country's premier player, the lanky golfer from Etobicoke who in his prime had such a sweet swing that even the great Sam Snead sought him out for practice rounds. But the Silver Fox, as he was called because of his full head of grey hair, played much of his career in an aura of tension, and he was the first to admit that he often didn't enjoy his game.

Al Balding was born in Toronto on April 29, 1924, and grew up as a kid of the depression. He quit school in Grade 7 and even though he had never golfed, one of his first jobs was caddying at the Islington course, close to his home. When Balding was 17, he was recognized as a hero; one night he noticed smoke coming out of a locked apartment. He smashed a glass door, opening up a gash on his arm, woke everyone up and made sure the building was evacuated.

At the time when the World War II was raging in Europe, Balding followed his friends and enlisted just before his 19th birthday. "When I joined up, I didn't figure to get in," recalled Balding in a 1977 profile in the *Globe and Mail*. "I was skinny, class B-1, and thought I'd wind up in the service corps. Instead I got into the artillery as a driver-mechanic."

Balding was shipped overseas and saw action in France and Germany as a member of the 13th Field Battery, 2nd Division. He was discharged just before the war ended when he hurt his shoulder. Balding said the injury was a result of fooling around on a motorcycle; something on the machine blew up, and the young serviceman ended up in a ditch.

"When I got out of the service, I couldn't even pitch a baseball. I went to building tires at Goodyear until I couldn't do that any more either."

Until the pain in his shoulder became too severe, Balding worked at the Goodyear Tire factory in the west end of Toronto, earning 6.2 cents a tire and building 145 tires a shift. He then became a transport truck driver for Carling O'Keefe, building up his arms by lifting up to 500 cases of beer a day.

Balding escaped the hard labour of the beer industry when he began working at a golf club in Burlington. He started hitting a few golf balls and soon discovered a passion for the game. In an interview with the *Toronto Star*, Balding described how he started to get hooked on golf.

"I can remember when I was cleaning clubs in Burlington we'd get one day off a week and I'd spend the whole day hitting balls. I just loved those rainy days when no one played, and I could go out and hit balls."

In 1949, he became a starter at the Oakdale Golf and Country Club. He earned $6.00 a day and bought his first set of clubs. At the age of 25, he started to get serious about his game. He developed his silky swing through hours of hard work and caught the eye of Les Franks, who at the time was one of Canada's finest teachers. Franks added the hard-working, six-foot-two former truck driver to his client list.

"I would pick up balls on the range to pay for a lesson which cost 15 cents," recalled Balding in a 1993 *Globe and Mail* profile by Lorne Rubenstein. "Les would whack a player's left knee to make sure it worked properly on the backswing, and insist he finish the swing with his elbows together."

Wardon Teasdale, a long-time friend of Balding's, recalled the magic touch Franks seemed to have with his young protégé: "One day Al went to Les complaining that his swing was giving him a little trouble. Franks sent a boy out on to the driving range, and Balding started pounding four-woods far down the range. The lad was walking just a few feet to his right or left each time to shag the balls."

"Balding shook his head at his lack of precision, 'See what I mean, Les?' The problem, such as it was, was quickly remedied. The boy hardly had to move a muscle after that as he collected the balls from Balding's drives."

Under Frank's tutelage, Balding put together a classic, sweeping, effortless swing. At the age of 26 he won the Ontario assistant pro championship. In 1954 he became the head professional at the Credit Valley Golf Club in Etobicoke. He entered Canadian events while keeping his head pro position at Credit Valley. As he became more experienced playing tournament golf, Balding improved to the point where he qualified to play on the PGA winter tour.

In December 1955, Balding became the first Canadian to win a professional event in the United States (Pat Fletcher won the Canadian Open the year before but it wasn't an official PGA Tour tournament), taking the Mayfair Inn Open in Miami. The Silver Fox had beaten a field that included Sam Snead and Tommy Bolt.

Two years later, Balding decided to tackle the U.S. Tour full time. With savings of $10,000 and another $8000 put up by a backer, Balding and his wife Moreen headed south.

He had immediate success with a swing that was one of the purest on the circuit. Even as a tall player, his swing had such rhythm that some big paydays seemed inevitable. In 1957, his first full year on the Tour, Balding won the Miami Beach Open, the West Palm Beach Open and the Havana Invitational. He finished sixth on the money list (Balding won $28,000; based on today's purses he would have earned $3.2 million), the highest standing of any Canadian until Mike Weir finished sixth in 2003.

A young George Knudson occasionally caddied for Balding that season. At a tournament in Los Angeles, Knudson spied the great Ben Hogan and suggested to his boss that they watch him finish his round. Balding looked at the sizable crowd following Hogan and replied, "To hell with that. Let them watch me."

Balding enjoyed great success in his first years on the Tour, but it was during an era before courtesy cars, endorsement deals or appearance money. He earned just $2100 for his first Tour win (a PGA win today offers a first place purse of at least $800,000). There was constant pressure to perform well, and during the inevitable slumps that all athletes suffer, things were sometimes lean at the Balding home.

"I've always had another job to do besides play golf, and I always worked hard at both," said Balding in describing how he made ends meet. "There were never enough hours in the day for me."

"From 1966 to 1968, I was pro at Markland Wood in the summer and Crystal River, Florida. I was playing Canadian golf in the summer and 15 U.S. winter tournaments, besides holding the two jobs."

The Silver Fox continued to make a decent living on the Tour through the 1960s. Besides the Canadian and PGA events, Balding played in Cuba, South America, Japan and Italy. He became known for his overall game; he wasn't an exceptional driver, iron guy or putter but could do everything decently well, and those overall skills benefited him on the course.

"He was a self-taught player," explained Karen Hewson, a former director of the Canadian Golf Hall of Fame. "He believed a lot in the feel of the game and was less obsessed with the mechanics. He was good at putting the whole game together."

His biggest international win came in 1968 when he teamed up with George Knudson to lead Canada to a World Cup Team Championship. Balding also won the individual trophy in the Rome event as low scorer over 72 holes. Back then the World Cup was one of golf's most prestigious events, and Balding's five-stroke victory made him the star of the tournament. The Balding-Knudson team defeated the best golfers in the world, including the American duo of Lee Trevino and Julius Boros.

Balding had battled back from a shoulder operation in 1965 to become an international champion. It was the first in the string of physical ailments and illnesses that slowed his progress as a dominant performer on the PGA Tour. The operations on his shoulder had to be repeated in 1970 and 1977.

After his World Cup victory in 1968, Balding sought to improve his game a notch by working with Toronto fitness expert Lloyd Percival. Even though the term "personal trainer" didn't exist, Balding found Percival's assistance invaluable in improving the way he felt on the course.

"It sounds odd," Balding said after losing 17 pounds on Percival's program, "but he helps you mentally as well as physically. I don't let things upset me anymore. I was even fairly calm when I broke my driver in the Westchester Classic."

Over the years Balding had gained a reputation as a cantankerous fellow, both on and off the course. "He was never one to mince words," said his old friend Teasdale. "It got him into trouble on occasion."

Teasdale recalled one charity event where a wealthy corporate type had paid a good sum of money to play a round with the Canadian professional. The guy hit the ball all over the course but kept telling Balding that he had taken lessons and had used this gizmo and that. When the round was finally over, the man looked at Balding and asked what he thought about his game. Balding replied bluntly, "When you get home you ought to package all that stuff up and ask for your money back."

"I've never smiled a lot, and I've never been one of those giggly guys," Balding once said. "I'm not really interested in being like that either."

"He was right to the point, off and on the course, and voiced his opinion so strongly and with such conviction," remembered Richard Zokol about the Canadian golfing legend. "He would never compromise what he had to say even if he broke some eggs."

Decades later Balding admitted that his own sensitive nature sometimes got in the way of him fully enjoying the company of others and in taking pleasure from the game itself. The Silver Fox, however, had to contend with several health issues that would have weighed on the most fun-loving of individuals.

Besides the wonky shoulder, in the mid-1970s, Balding was diagnosed with blood cancer, a rare type of the disease. The prognosis was not good as most people die within two or three years, but he battled through the illness, taking 16 pills a day for years. He had to undergo annual bone marrow tests and at times take medication to balance his white and red blood cells.

"The doctors tell me that the cancer is in slumber," Balding explained. "But it's always there. I have it and it's been controlled. I was lucky, maybe because it was caught early."

In later years, he underwent quadruple bypass surgery, had a pacemaker installed and had eye surgery. Despite the severity of his health issues, Balding came back to play some amazing tournament golf. In the 1970s, he became one of the founding members of the Senior PGA Tour—now the Champions Tour. In 1985, the 61-year-old Balding finished 21st on the Senior money list, ahead of younger legends Gary Player, Chi Chi Rodriguez and Doug Sanders.

Part of his late success had to do with letting go of the tension that was omnipresent with each round of golf. He began seeing a therapist to begin the process of letting go of all the baggage that he carried during each competitive round. He learned to think only of relaxing on the course, of playing the game subconsciously and not getting caught up in the mechanics of the swing.

"I can relax at will now most of the time," said Balding. "I relax my eyes and get a warm sensation from the eyelids down. The feeling goes right through my whole body. I still can't do it with my putting as well as I would like, but it's coming. I probably try too hard."

By 1991, Balding had lost his playing card for the Seniors Tour by finishing out of the top 50 on the money list. In 1992, he tied for third in a Phoenix tournament billed as golf's field of dreams. Balding pocketed $8500, his biggest paycheque in years. In 1994, he notched his first victory on the Senior Tour, winning the Liberty

Mutual Legends of Golf Championship with partner Jay Hebert.

Balding made headlines around the golfing world in 2000, when at age 76, he won the 2000 Canadian PGA Seniors' Championship. The Silver Fox fired three consecutive two-under-par rounds of 70, to beat his closest contender (who was 26 years younger) by three strokes. When asked by reporters afterwards how he managed to shoot a better score than golfers much younger, Balding dryly replied, "How old would you be if you didn't know how old you are?

Even though Balding had been very active in Canadian golfing circles, the victory brought him overdue exposure to a new generation of players. Even a year later he was asked about his victory, "I got more recognition out of that win than I had in years,"

The following year at another senior event, Balding received more notice when he had a round of 66, 12 shots lower than his age. PGA historians said the feat was unparalleled in tournament golf.

Balding was a much mellower guy on and off the course, though he could still be outspoken if he deemed an issue needed to be aired. In the late 1970s, he publicly declared his disgust at the deterioration of Canadian golf.

"I can't understand it. There were more Canadians on the big tour when I played than there are now, and we're supposed to have advanced. What have we got, George Knudson? One guy, 40 years old, and he's not playing regularly."

To his credit Balding tried to improve Canadian golf, first by becoming a respected teacher of the game, as a golf director at the National Golf Club and then by forming an institute to run clinics across the country to help young professionals trying to qualify for the Canadian Tour.

Balding's blunt assessment of the Canadian golfing establishment delayed some of the recognition he had so well deserved, such as when the Royal Canadian Golf Association did not admit him to its Hall of Fame until 1985. Balding's feelings were hurt, and he spoke emotionally about the slight.

"I never knew why it took so long," he said in 1993. "After all, only a few Canadians won tournaments in the United States. I was the only one to finish in the top 10 on the Tour, and George and I were the first to win the World Cup for Canada."

Even after his inclusion into the Hall, Balding didn't soften much. In 1996 he publicly reamed out the RCGA when he wasn't granted a sponsor's exemption to play in the $1.1 million du Maurier Senior Champions event in Hamilton.

The Silver Fox, then 72, was bypassed to allow Bob Wylie, the Canadian Amateur Seniors champ to play.

"I'm really disappointed in what they've done," said Balding. "They [the RCGA] said they invited Bob Wylie because he won the Canadian Amateur Seniors. Well, so what? What's the Canadian Amateur Seniors?"

In 2006, at the age of 82, Balding finally lost his decades-long battle with cancer. His many friends acknowledged the crusty side of the Silver Fox, but they also shared stories of his generosity and warmth.

"He was a great guy," said Mike Weir. "I spent a little bit of time with Al when I was playing the Canadian Tour. I had a lot of great conversations with him."

Bill (Skip) Johns, a sports reporter for over 45 years in southern Ontario remembered a chance encounter with Balding on the golf course.

Johns and a buddy were heading for the 10th hole when the golfing legend walked over from the practice green and asked if he could play the back nine with them. A few holes later, both Johns and his friend hit into a bunker and made terrible shots trying to get out of the sand. Balding had been waiting patiently on the green, but finally strode over and told both men to get a half-dozen golf balls out of their bags. For the next 45 minutes, he gave an impromptu lesson on sand play as they let other groups play through.

Gary McKay, a sports columnist with the *Hamilton Spectator* remembered another unscripted Balding moment at the 1974 Ontario Open. McKay had been covering the tournament and was in the concession tent having a drink, when a golf ball came bouncing in. A group of marshals made sure no one stepped on it, and a few minutes later, Balding came striding in.

The Silver Fox joked about wanting to play through, and after a short discussion, it was decided he would be allowed relief. The marshals told him where to drop the ball, placing him behind the tent so he would have to shoot blind to the green.

"He executed the shot perfectly and two putted for par," recalled McKay. "I remembered thinking, This guy's good."

Chapter Fourteen

Moe Norman
Canada's Golf Savant

Born Kitchener, Ontario, 1929–2004

Before his death in 2004, Moe Norman was the most colourful personality in Canadian golf. His legacy is confirmed not by PGA Tour victories, amateur titles or money earnings. Moe Norman will be remembered for his ability to hit amazing golf shots. Lee Trevino said he was the best ball striker he had ever seen.

The legend of Moe Norman is built on golf shots and the stories that came out of those shots. In 1995, author Tim O'Connor compiled some of the most famous tales in *The Feeling of Greatness: The Moe Norman Story*.

During a practice round at the 1971 Canadian Open, reporters questioned Norman about his poor putting at a previous event as he walked to the 10th tee. Norman didn't say a word, grabbed his driver and bashed a shot at the par 3, 233-yard hole. As the ball sailed towards the green, he turned around, looked at the reporters and said: "I'm not putting today." The ball landed inches from the cup and rolled in.

During a golf clinic at a driving range in Florida, Norman's friend Ken Venning, dropped a small ball bag a 100 yards away. He told the gallery that he would donate $5.00 every time Moe hit the bag. Using every club from wedge to driver, Norman nailed the bag. At $100, Venning told him to stop.

At another clinic in Florida, Moe told the crowd that things would begin at a practice green 85 yards away. To point out the spot, Norman hit his first shot into the hole.

Former NHL all-star Stan Mikita remembered playing with Norman at a club in St. Catharine's, Ontario. On the ninth tee, Moe asked Mikita what clubs he would use on the 400-yard par 4. The hockey legend replied, "a drive and a wedge." Norman hit a wedge 130 yards and then ripped the driver about three feet from the hole.

Moe Norman became a master of ball striking by hitting a lot of balls; he set a minimum of 600 per day. As a youngster he hit up to 1500 balls in a single session, only darkness, physical exhaustion or sore hands sent him home.

Norman didn't wear a glove. Typically his hands would sting and then blister; the skin would peel back and then came the blood. As his hands became slippery, he would wipe the blood on his pants. Eventually he developed thick, dark calluses that he would have to cut back with razor blades so he could hold the club naturally.

All in all, Moe Norman could be an intimidating presence in the cultured atmosphere of a golf club. He usually wore a long-sleeved turtleneck that accented a powerful chest and thick neck. His face always looked sunburned, the wide jaw holding a thin mouth full of crooked teeth. Norman's thick, grey eyebrows shot upwards when he listened, and his blue eyes widened in an expression of amazement. As he aged, he clipped his grey hair short at the sides, but wild tufts often escaped to stick out in all directions.

His social mannerisms also added to his wild-man look. Norman spoke as rapidly as he hit golf balls and often repeated himself. His voice was high-pitched, Winnie the Pooh-like in tone. He gave free golf balls to little children, but often angrily snapped at adults who asked for an autograph. He often walked away from reporters, and if they persisted, he would blast them with a torrent of profanity. He hid at trophy presentations. He never smoked, took an alcoholic drink or went on a date.

For decades he was estranged from his family, erroneously thinking that they hated his passion for golf. He faced poverty on several occasions. His possessions fit in the trunk of his car. He rented rooms most of his life, but only a few close friends knew where. He never had a phone or a credit card.

Moe Norman was an eccentric dedicated to a single pursuit, to hit perfect golf shots. He was a maverick who developed his own swing—an awkward sequence of movements that started with a stance where his legs were spread wide and rigidly straight. His arms were also stretched out, as unyielding as his legs, and his elbows were locked. His big hands seemed to smother the shaft of the club with a vice-like grip that prevented the club from wavering.

Norman's wide stance was not built for power, rather it was designed for accuracy. His back-swing was short and restrained, barely taking the club back to a three-quarter position. To further command each swing, Norman gripped down about three inches from the butt end of his grip; this too sacrificed distance for accuracy, but with his powerful Popeye arms, Norman could still knock the ball a long way.

Murray "Moe" Norman and his twin sister Marie were born on July 10, 1929, in Kitchener, Ontario. Murray was one of six children. His father was a quiet, stern-looking man. The kids were like their father, subdued and withdrawn. The Normans were a struggling working-class family with eight people stuffed into a three-bedroom house.

When he was five years old, Murray and a friend were zipping down a hill on a toboggan. A long flat zone between the bottom of the hill and a local road usually offered lots of buffer distance from traffic, but on this day the hill was sheet ice, and the toboggan went into the path of an oncoming car. The sleigh disappeared under the front wheels of the vehicle. The driver lost control, and the car crashed into the veranda of a house on the street.

The boys had been carried about 30 metres under the car. A few moments passed and then they appeared, pulling themselves from underneath the vehicle. They were shaken, but except for minor cuts and bruises, were apparently unharmed. The driver of the vehicle pleaded with Murray's mother, Mary to take Murray to the hospital, but back then there was no national health insurance. It was the Depression, and money was tight.

Inevitably, later on in life, Murray Norman's eccentric behaviour, his rapid speaking and repetition of speech were linked to a possible brain injury from the accident. His brothers and sisters were too young to remember the incident, but there is some agreement that he was never treated properly for his injuries.

However, the release of the movie *The Rain Man* in 1988 changed people's thinking. Norman's eccentric behaviour was amazingly similar to Dustin Hoffman's portrayal of a middle-aged autistic man. Friends and physicians were certain that Norman was an autistic savant, a term coined for autistics who often have exceptional math, memory or music skills.

He showed a remarkable agility with numbers. His card counting ability made him almost unbeatable at poker. He could remember the number of courses he'd played in his lifetime (434) and in most cases (375), the exact hole yardages. Norman was never tested for autism (he didn't trust doctors), but he kept a crumpled article about the neurological condition on the front seat of his Cadillac.

By the time he reached the age of 12, golf had seeped into Murray's life, first as a caddie at the Westmount Golf and Country Club. Thursday was caddie's day, and Norman began skipping school to play. Quickly, the game became an obsession, and Murray, who had now been nicknamed "Moe" by the other caddies, began playing every day during the summer months at Rockway, a public course in Kitchener.

Norman was not a natural golfer, but the sport became his vocation. He spent hours improving his swing, and by the time he was 17, he was shooting in the 70s. At 19 he won his first tournament. A year later, Norman had saved enough money to pay the entry fee to play in amateur tournaments around the province. He began winning invitational tourneys and one-day events.

News of his ball-striking abilities spread, and Moe didn't disappoint the fans. He began hitting the ball off of a series of high tees, including an eight-inch colossus. Once he entertained a gallery by bouncing the ball off his club 184 times straight without it touching the ground. He played so fast that at times it seemed he was hitting the ball in mid stride.

Norman played the amateur circuit full time during the golf season, winning two-thirds of the 30 events he entered. Amateur golfers weren't expected to make a living playing golf. Moe survived by sleeping outside, eating junk food and selling the prizes he won at tournaments, a violation of the amateur rules.

"Hell, all I ever seemed to win were TV sets," he told one journalist. "One year I had six, so

I sold them. They said I couldn't. I said, 'What am I supposed to do, watch all six?' They said, 'Yes.'"

Moe made ends meet by playing in exhibition games at the clubs he visited, often pocketing a couple of hundred dollars under the table. For the big events that required Norman to travel outside the province, a number of Rockway members would take up a collection so he could make the trip.

By 1954, Norman was the number-one ranked amateur in Ontario. It was the start of a wonderful run for the shy young man from Kitchener. The next year he travelled to Calgary and won the Canadian Amateur title in a thrilling 39-hole match play victory over Lyle Crawford from Vancouver. Moe hid just before the trophy presentation, forcing Crawford to thank the crowd on his behalf.

Norman's victory meant an invitation to the Masters. Not surprisingly, he hit every ball straight, but his nerves caught up to him on the greens. Moe three-putted six times and ended up shooting a 75. Things didn't improve the next day when he shot a 78. After the round, Norman went to the practice range to get ready for day three (there was no cut in the Masters back then). The legendary Sam Snead began watching the young Canadian, introduced himself and offered some swing advice to improve his iron play.

Moe took Snead's words to heart and was determined to master his tip. For the rest of the afternoon and into the evening, he hit shot after shot, 800 balls in all. His hands were raw and red by the end of the session. The next day he could barely hold the club, and after nine holes, he had to withdraw from the tournament.

In 1956 he defended his Canadian Amateur title. He had to give up a night job fixing tires to make the trip to New Brunswick. There should have been a celebration in recognition of Norman's back-to-back victories, but nobody made the trip to Toronto to greet him at the airport.

"I flew back to Toronto with Jerry Magee, the guy I'd beaten," related Norman in a *Maclean's* magazine profile. "No one was there to meet me. No one. But people came to meet Jerry. His parents were there with the keys to a brand new Oldsmobile. It was raining out, raining hard, and I had to go up to Jerry and ask him if I could hitch a ride with him out to Highway 7, so I could hitchhike back to Kitchener. Jerry took me out in the new car and dumped me off. I was standing there with my clubs and this great big trophy, and Jerry drives off in this new Olds."

Norman's battle with the Royal Canadian Golf Association over selling prize gifts and conducting paid exhibitions intensified. In the first week of 1957, he turned professional. However, without a Canadian Professional Golf Association card or a U.S. PGA card, Norman was not qualified to play in their events.

He headed south, playing the odd "open" tournament in Georgia and Florida. He became good at golf "hustling"— winning bets against well-heeled country club members. He was a natural as a golf hustler. With his unkempt appearance and eccentric mannerisms, his competitors were seldom tipped off that a scratch golfer was lurking to take their money.

In 1958 he signed on as an assistant pro at the ritzy de Havilland Golf Centre in Toronto. He worked out a deal that allowed Norman to receive his CPGA tour card in return for teaching, appearing at golfing exhibitions and representing de Havilland at tournaments. He won his first big paycheque a few months later, pocketing $1000 by winning the Ontario Open. Later that summer, Norman finished in the top three in a bursary tournament (an event for young professionals to earn some money to further their pro careers), making him eligible to play in the PGA winter tour.

Norman's arrival on the 1959 PGA Tour was much anticipated by fans in Canada. Moe had learned to drive during the winter and bought a brown Coupe de Ville Cadillac. PGA officials had been warned about Norman's on-course antics and told the rookie golfer that they would not tolerate any "shenanigans."

It was a tough go for the Canadian to fit in with his fellow pros. He amazed the other players with his shot-making abilities and his work ethic, but he kept to himself, especially around the top players. On the course, he had all the shots, except on the putting green. Putting was never a skill that Norman was much interested in mastering. He never lingered over a putt, it was the one place on the golf course where everything slowed down, and Moe never liked to be on stage too long.

His best finish on the Tour that year was in the 1959 Greater New Orleans Open. Norman was three strokes back of Gene Littler going into the final day after rounds of 70-72-70. Norman shot a 72 in the final round to finish fourth, pocketing $1100. In 10 events during the winter tour he managed to win only $1360 before heading back to de Havilland for another season.

In 1960, Norman again qualified to play on the PGA Tour. He pocketed only $1530 despite making the cut in all 10 events. By keeping his expenses down, Moe broke even, but he'd had enough. After the last event, he decided to come home for good. Norman's friends all had different explanations for his decision to leave the PGA Tour—boredom, loneliness, a lack of financial success.

With his dream of getting rich playing golf in the United States now history, Norman became a teaching pro. He still played pro tournaments in Canada and made extra money with his ball-striking exhibitions.

He found the time to win over 50 tournaments, set 33 course records, including three sanctioned scores of 59. Throw in 17 career holes-in-one and nine double eagles, and the legend of Moe Norman only grew bigger. In 1966, he enjoyed his finest year as a pro when he won five of the 12 tournaments he entered, came in second five times and finished no lower than fifth. When Norman turned 50 in 1979, he won seven consecutive Canadian PGA senior championships. One of his sanctioned 59s came at the age of 62.

The other side of Moe was still ever-present. He routinely drank 24 Cokes a day. He hid huge sums of money in his Cadillac (he didn't have a bank account until late in life) in rolled-up wads of hundred-dollar bills. Sometimes he wore three watches on his left arm, all set to the same time.

In the early 1980s, he began to struggle in tournament play. He sank into debt, at one point owing close to $20,000. In 1986, the members of

Kitchener's Westmount Golf Club put on a Moe Norman Appreciation Day and raised $26,000. In front of a large audience, Moe gave the speech of his life, poetic and heartfelt words that had his friends both laughing and moved to tears. With the money he was able to pay his bills.

Things began to turn around as Norman began to receive recognition for his great talent. CBC-TV's current affairs show *The Fifth Estate* ran a profile on Moe and the U.S. golf magazine *GOLF* did a major piece. He was also approached to make an instructional video.

Things were still financially tough for Norman until 1995 when Titleist chairman Wally Uihlein announced that in recognition of his contribution to golf, his company was going to give Moe a $5000 monthly stipend for the rest of his life. In return, Norman volunteered to give some clinics and be filmed for instructional videos. He was inducted into the Canadian Golf Hall of Fame that same year.

As Moe slowed down, the highlight of his year would be showing up at the practice range during the Canadian Open. He would chat with the pros and begin hitting balls. Inevitably he drew a crowd; Mike Weir, Tom Watson, Fred Couples, Nick Faldo and the other top professionals would watch in awe as he hit ball after ball, straight and true.

Just before the 2004 Canadian Open, Moe passed away from heart failure at the age of 75. Over 450 people filled a church in Waterloo to pay their respects. Not surprisingly, his friends and family shared "Moe" stories, often not about his golf talent but anecdotes about his generosity and good humour.

An old friend, Garry Slatter, recalled playing with Moe during the 1971 Québec Open near Montréal: "We had a good crowd with us, and when we teed off I told Moe I thought I was going to play better than him. He said if I played better than him, then I'd have more money than him, and then he pulls out that big wad [of money], shows everybody and knocks me down, grabbing me by my ankles and shaking me upside down. 'Let's see what you got in your pockets...'"

The crowd ate it up.

Appendix: Player Records

Ames, Stephen
Years on PGA Tour: 13
Tour wins: 4
Total earnings: $17,992,396 (39th)

Balding, Al
Years on PGA Tour: 15
Tour wins: 4
Total earnings: $168,446 (835th)

Barr, Dave
Years on PGA Tour: 24
Tour wins: 2
Total earnings: $2,404,793(288th)

Coe-Jones, Dawn
Years on LPGA Tour: 24
Tour wins: 3
Total earnings: $3,315,477 (50th)

Graham, Gail
Years on LPGA Tour: 14
Tour wins: 2
Total earnings: $1,285,769 (142nd)

Kane, Lorie
Years on LPGA Tour: 14
Tour wins: 4
Total earnings: $6,716,288(15th)

Knudson, George
Years on PGA Tour: 11
Tour wins: 8
Total earnings: $532,137 (591st)

Leggatt, Ian
Years on PGA Tour: 7
Tour wins: 1
Total earnings: $2,870,906 (286th)

Leonard, Stan
Years on PGA Tour: 9
Tour wins: 3
Total earnings: $96,968 (969th)

Nelford, Jim
Years on PGA Tour: 13
Tour wins: 0
Total earnings: $485,111(602nd)

Norman, Moe
Years on PGA Tour: 2
Tour wins: 0
Total earnings: $2,890

Post, Sandra
Years on LPGA Tour: 17
Tour wins: 8
Total earnings: $746,714 (222nd)

Walters, Lisa
Years on LPGA Tour: 17
Tour wins: 3
Total earnings: $1,049,068(171st)

Weir, Mike
Years on PGA Tour: 13
Tour wins: 8
Total earnings: $26,239,282 (11th)

Wyatt, Jennifer
Years on LPGA Tour: 10
Tour wins: 1
Total earnings: $372,471 (162nd)

Zokol, Richard
Years on PGA Tour: 17
Tour wins: 2
Total earnings: $1,840,397(325th)

Notes on Sources

Barclay, James A. *Golf in Canada: A History*. Toronto: McClelland and Stewart, 1992.

Feinstein, John. *The Majors*. Boston: Little, Brown and Company, 1999.

Knudson, George with Lorne Rubenstein. *The Natural Golf Swing*. Toronto: McClelland and Stewart, 1988.

Nelford, Jim with Lorne Rubenstein. *Seasons in a Golfer's Life*. Agincourt, Ontario: Methuen Publications, 1984.

O'Connor, Tim. *The Feeling of Greatness: The Moe Norman Story*. Indianapolis: Masters Press, 1995.

Olson, Arv. *Backspin: 100 Years of Golf in British Columbia*. Altona, Manitoba: Friesen Printers, 1992.

Rubenstein, Lorne. *Touring Prose: Writings on Golf*. Toronto: Random House, 1992.

Rubenstein, Lorne. *Mike Weir: The Road to the Masters*. Toronto: McClelland and Stewart, 2003.

Weir, Mike with Tim Campbell and Scott Morrison. *On Course with Mike Weir*. Toronto: McGraw-Hill Ryerson Ltd., 2001.

Web Sources

"A Blast from the Past," June 24, 1985. wwwsportsillustrated.com. Retrieved August 24, 2009.

"A Long Road to Augusta," April 17, 1995. wwwsportsillustrated.com. Retrieved August 31, 2009.

"Ames Captures Players Championship Title," March 27, 2006. www.tsn.ca. Retrieved September 15, 2009.

Hall of Fame Profiles (n.d.) www.rcga.org. Retrieved May 18, 2009.

"Leggatt Claims First PGA Tour Win" (n.d.) www.golftoday.co.uk. Retrieved September 1, 2009.

Leggatt Interview, August 11, 2006. www.asapsports. mobi. Retrieved September 1, 2009.

Leggatt Returns to Canada, September 5, 2006. www.pga-tour.com. Retrieved September 1, 2009.

Mike Weir (n.d.)www.mikeweir.com. Retrieved September 21, 2009.

Player Profiles (n.d.) www.lpga.com. Retrieved May 18, 2009.

Presidents Cup Recap, September 30, 2007. www.sports. espn.go.com. Retrieved October 7, 2009.

Sandra Post Golf School (n.d.) www.sandrapost.ca. Retrieved July 15, 2009.

Stephen Ames, March 1, 2008. www.fairwaygolf.com. Retrieved September 15, 2009.

"Stephen Ames Coasts to Six Shot Win" (n.d.). www. golftoday.co.uk. Retrieved June 14, 2009.

"Unfinished Business for Weir," July 21, 2008.www. sportsnet.ca. Retrieved June 14, 2009.

"Weir and Wonderful," April 23, 2003. www.sportsillus-trated.cnn.com. Retrieved September 18, 2009.

Information was also used from the following print outlets:

Alberta Report, Calgary Herald, Calgary Sun, Canadian Business, Edmonton Journal, Globe and Mail, Golf Canada, Golf Digest, GolfDigest.com magazine, *Hamilton Spectator, Maclean's* magazine, *Montreal Gazette, National Post, Ottawa Citizen, The Record,* SCOREGolf.com magazine, *Toronto Star, USA Today, Vancouver Province, Vancouver Sun, Waterloo Chronicle, Weekend Magazine, Windsor Star, Winnipeg Free Press.*

Stephen Drake

Stephen Drake was born in Vancouver and grew up on a ranch near Merritt, BC. His love for golf started as a teenager when he spent many carefree summer days at the Quilchena Golf Course beside Nicola Lake. Six dollars was all it took to have free rein on the nine-hole layout—the course emptied out in the scorching heat of the afternoon. These days Stephen is a freelance writer, sharing space with his wife and two children. He is the author of three other non-fiction sports titles for OverTime Books.